A NATION OF GARDENERS

How the British Fell in Love with Gardening

Twigs Way

PRION

This is Prion book

Text & Design © Carlton Books Limited 2010

Garden Museum logo © The Garden Museum 2010

This edition published in 2010 by Prion
A division of the Carlton Publishing Group
20 Mortimer Street
London
W1T 3JW

Printed in Dubai

A CIP catalogue for this book is available from the British Library

ISBN: 978-1-85375-806-5

This book is dedicated to Teasal (2001–2010) who loved to garden

ABOVE: Pottering in the greenhouse is a national obsession, captured here by David Rose (c. 1930).

OPPOSITE: This early eighteenth-century pen-and-ink sketch shows a "lost garden" with its summerhouse and water feature.

Author's Acknowledgements
A book is always a collaborative effort, regardless of whose name is on the title page. This book would never have been possible without the commitment and enthusiasm of Philip Norman, Voluntary Assistant Curator of the Garden Museum. Philip's thorough knowledge of the Museum's collections resulted in the wealth of illustrative material and made writing the book a pleasure. Production was also generously assisted by Christopher Woodward, Director of the Garden Museum, and Mary Guyatt, Curator. I would also like to thank Brent Elliott, Head Librarian of the RHS Lindley Library for, as ever, answering questions with prompt efficiency and astounding breadth of knowledge. My garden history colleague, Caroline Holmes, also answered queries and checked details. Vanessa Daubney at Carlton Books remained remarkably calm and supportive as deadlines came (and went). As always, I would not have been able to devote time to writing the book without the help of my partner, Steve Kemp, who yet again took on all the other duties of life, not least the gardening!

Contents

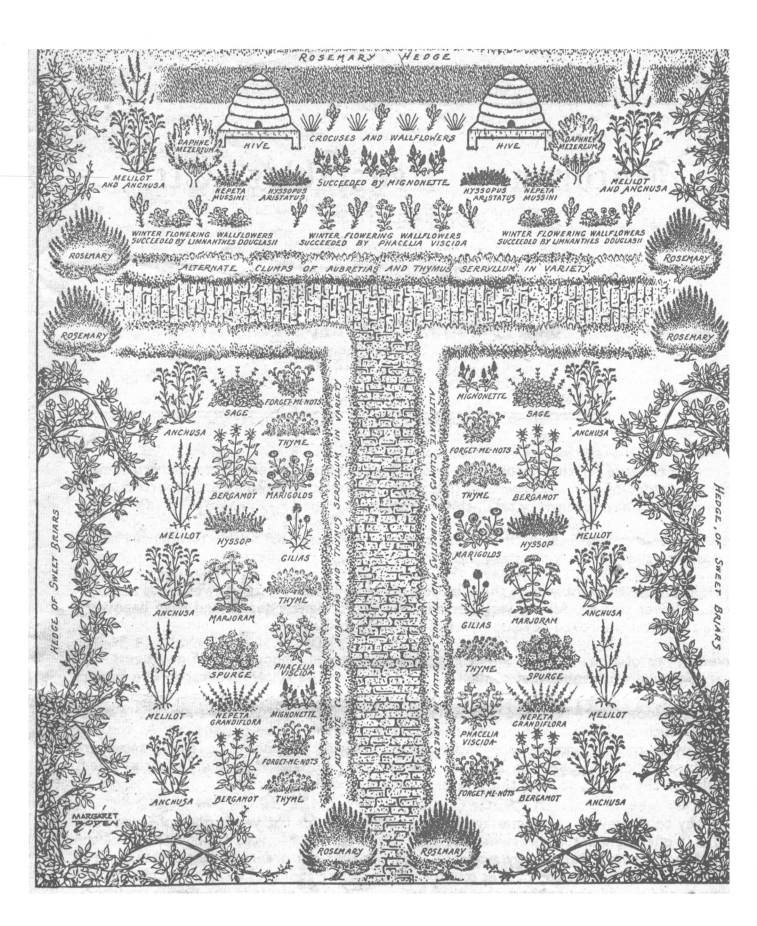

Foreword

by Joe Swift

We British are internationally famed for being passionate gardeners, but sometimes it's difficult to explain precisely why. I've been asked by foreign magazines and TV programmes just what it is about the Brits and their gardens? Why do we do it? Where does our love for plants come from and why do we feel the need to stamp our personalities all over our plots whatever shape and size they may be?

Well, they obviously don't quite get it or they wouldn't be asking the question in the first place. I'd make a stab at a brief answer, muttering something about a combination of elements. It's our climate, our soil, our love of travel, our social and economic history and, of course, a healthy but yes, perhaps a little eccentric, obsession for all things horticultural be it edible or ornamental. In future, I don't think I'll bother answering. I'll just hand them a copy of *A Nation of Gardeners* and if that doesn't get them going and help them to understand our inherent passion and desire to get out and garden, then nothing will.

In this wonderful book Twigs Way has captured a huge amount of our absorbing gardening heritage and history, yet there's no lecturing going on here. Relevant anecdotes, quotations and captions are elegantly knitted together in her approachable, upbeat style. I adore the vibrant imagery throughout; tools, posters, periodicals, photos, toys, advertisements, cartoons and postcards introduce visual detail that words alone cannot capture, igniting each page and drawing you deeper into each subject and era.

I'm a regular visitor to the Garden Museum and delighted that some of their comprehensive archive can now be appreciated by a wider audience. Some are extremely useful, too, such as the "Dig for Victory" vegetable planner. It's just as relevant today with our renewed interest in grow your own and, if you follow it season by season, you won't go far wrong. There's something comforting in knowing that most of our current gardening techniques have been used for decades in some form or other. Some simple tools, a few seeds and a patch of soil or even a pot or two and off you go. Gardening knows few barriers. Class, age, gender, ability and cultures are unified through gardening. It's something we are particularly good at, should be proud of and *A Nation of Gardeners* celebrates that sentiment wholeheartedly.

What a wonderful book.

Joe Swift

OPPOSITE: The garden designer and historian Eleanour Sinclair Rhode (1881–1950) specialised in herbs and unusual vegetables, anticipating a revival of interest in the late twentieth century.

Introduction

"God Almighty first planted a garden; and, indeed, it is the purest of human pleasures ... men come to build stately sooner than to garden finely; as if gardening were the greater perfection." So wrote Francis Bacon, the English essayist, in 1625. Almost four hundred years later the gardeners of England, and for that matter the rest of the United Kingdom, still strive for that perfection, giving birth to the adage that we are a "Nation of Gardeners".

But how did we arrive at this floral image of ourselves and our small island "hedged in with the main", as Shakespeare so aptly describes us? When did we first start to we perfect our small plots and re-arrange our landscapes, giving Dame Nature a helping hand where she fell short of our horticultural ideals? Even within our small islands our garden fashions seem to continually change, so that the formal is followed by the informal, only to find itself transformed, yet again, into gardens of militaristic precision. One generation's Garden of Eden is, it seems, another generation's biblical Land of Nod, a place of wretched wilderness and wanderings. Perfection seems forever just beyond our grasp.

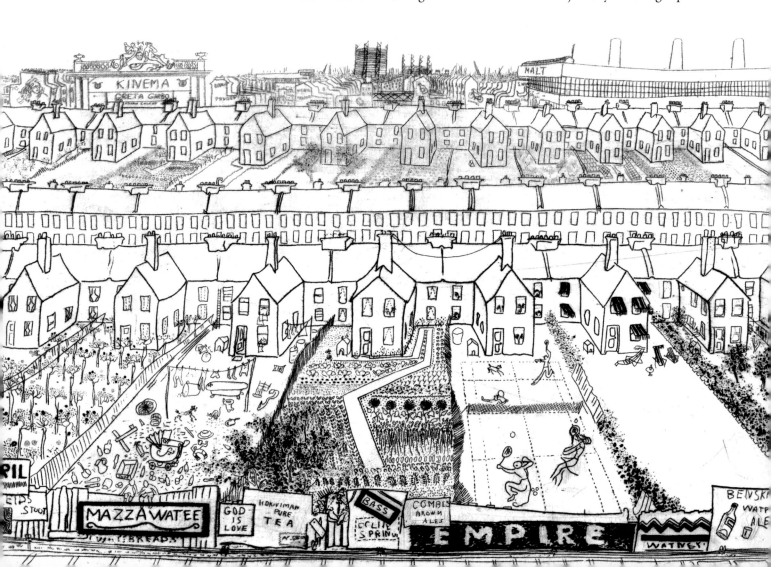

And so we start again, planting and re-planting, and even, in the words of the eighteenth-century garden creator, Lady Luxborough, "displanting"!

A recent survey by the National Trust revealed that over 70 per cent of people felt it was important to spend time in gardens, and over half of those said it was the most enjoyable thing they did. A third of those surveyed even revealed that time spent amongst the flower borders boosted their love life! Horticulture has us hooked. Even when we are not in the garden, we are visiting gardens. Almost 4,000 gardens open to the public under the National Gardens Scheme (known as the Yellow Book because of its once challengingly bright cover) and more join every year. Historic gardens are lovingly restored and recreated by bodies such as the National Trust and English Heritage, and volunteers flock to lend a hand, planting their own bit of history for the future.

Gardens, after all, are not just about plants; they are about people. It is people who make a garden and care for it, people who invent tools to use in the garden, who discover exotic new plants, sell seeds and bulbs, design new glasshouses, and dictate new fashions. People play in gardens as children, support the nation through war in their garden, make their living from gardens, and even write about gardens.

Using the unique archives of the Garden Museum, this book explores the history behind the fashions and the fantasies, from the humble medieval vegetable plot to the Chelsea Flower Show, from working-class allotments to gardening for royalty. Garden writers, garden designers and garden owners fill its pages, peering out from long forgotten photographs, proudly clasping a lawnmower, a spade or a watering can. Caught in the act of beautifying their plot, they bring to life the story of our nation, the nation of gardeners.

ABOVE: This unusual image is the garden of the religious sect founded by the Reverend Henry Prince in 1846 at Spraxtion, Somerset. They called themselves the Family of Love, and the gardens andhouse were the Abode of Love.

OPPOSITE: Anthony Gross's delightful etching, entitled *South London*, provides a rare glimpse of suburban back gardens inthe 1930s, demonstrating the variety with which we fill our "plots".

A Garden Is a Lovesome Thing

As the ice sheets rolled back from a wet and chilly Britain some 12,000 years ago, there were only about 200 species of plants left standing, and most of those would be regarded as distinctly unpromising by the average gardener. Imagine arriving at the local garden centre to find your choice restricted to some low-growing insect-eating plants, bilberry bushes and a handful of small and insignificantly flowered relatives of the *Alchemilla*, and you can understand why gardening got off to a slow start. In fact, the only flower that might find its place in a flower border today was the dainty wild violet, *Viola rupestris*. Admittedly there were 35 species of tree to choose from, but few of those (yew, juniper and holly) were evergreen, so things looked pretty bleak for anyone with an eye to "year-round design". A decent hedge could theoretically have been made around prehistoric habitations with the handy native box (*Buxus sempervirens*), had anyone had the ability to make shears or the time to wield them, but archaeology suggests that this particular garden feature had to await the arrival of the Romans. Our European neighbours had a more favourable start in their gardening endeavours, with almost twice as many native plants in France, perhaps making our own eventual achievements all the more notable! As the climate ameliorated over the centuries, the number of species increased, both on purpose and by accident. Settlers from the Continent brought plants they were used to using for medicines and foods. Domestic crops arrived, and with them the inevitable weeds. Our landscape began to fill. But it is to the Romans that we owe the first real influx of gardens and garden plants, another in the long list of replies to that *Monty Python* query "What have the Romans ever done for us?".

From a gardening point of view, the Romans found Britain distinctly challenging. The weather was unpropitious, being memorably described by one Roman writer as "unpleasant, with frequent rain and mist", although he added

A GARDEN IS A LOVESOME THING

optimistically that it did not suffer from extreme cold and had a fertile soil. All crops might be grown there, he added, apart from those that required warmer climes. Unfortunately this last caveat excluded many of the Romans' favourite plants: olives, vines, figs and the drought-loving Mediterranean herbs such as hyssop, thyme and rosemary. Undeterred, the Romans promptly imported all of these. Armed with seeds, cuttings and optimism, they commenced beautifying the surroundings to their villas, and the fashion soon caught on. Fishbourne Roman "Palace" (near Chichester, Sussex) was first excavated by archaeologists in the 1960s and several seasons of work revealed a large formal garden with subsidiary formal and productive gardens. The main formal garden, measuring some 245 x 295 feet (75 x 90 metres), drew the astounded visitor in to this outpost of Roman culture, along a wide path edged with double and triple lines of clipped box hedging, flanking lawns relieved with large trees and probably containing statues in its alcoves. We know little about what flowers were grown here, but other sites have revealed that Roman towns in Britain made a show of roses, mallows and aquilegias. Cultivated apples, walnuts, quince and sweet chestnut were all added to our native diet, alongside carrots, peas, a type of parsnip, mulberries, cucumbers, garlic, onions, asparagus, radishes, hops and hemp. One begins to wonder what we ate before. Spades, billhooks, hoes, scythes and rakes were all introduced, or improved by the addition of metal edges allowing the tending of these new arrivals. Only the fork and the vine-dressers' tools were missing.

As the Romans retreated in the fifth century, they left behind them some of the new skills they had brought: the grafting of trees and vines, layering of shrubs and herbs, clipping of topiary, manuring and even rudimentary attempts at forcing – using warm water on the roots or wheeling plants in and out to catch the precious rays of sunshine. Alas, there is little evidence that anyone put these into practice during the long centuries that followed, and England entered a gardening wilderness.

We pick up our story again in the thirteenth century, with a royal garden created for, or perhaps by, Queen Eleanor of Provence. There is little evidence of her husband, Henry III, having any interest in gardens, but from her cultured Provençal background Eleanor would have been familiar with Continental gardens, and so it is no surprise to find instructions issued in 1250 for the making of "two good high walls around the garden of the Queen so that no one may be able to enter, with a becoming and pleasant herbary near the King's fish-pond in which the same Queen may be able to enjoy herself … and with a gate from the herbary … into the aforesaid garden". Within this enclosed garden there would by now have been many additions to our limited native plants, such as pinks, cowslips, dog roses, honeysuckle and violets. Later, the quince tree is supposed to have been re-introduced by her daughter-in-law, Queen Eleanor of Castile. Eleanor is also credited with bringing back the the hollyhock on her return from the crusades, giving it its name "holy-hock". A final touch to the garden's beauties would

ABOVE: The mandrake root, with its supposed resemblance to the human figure, was thought to scream when it was uprooted, sending anyone that heard it insane.

BELOW: Ceramic watering pots had pierced bases. The pot was filled by dipping it in a bowl of water and then made tight by putting a thumb over the top so that no water could come out of the base. Once the pot was in position over the plants, the thumb could be removed, air rushed in and water streamed out of the pierced base.

ABOVE: Good King Henry and salad burnet were popular plants in the peasant's vegetable plot. Here they have been grown at the Prebendal Manor Garden, Nassington, Northamptonshire.

BELOW: Leek planting has not changed over the centuries, although gardeners' dress has.

BELOW RIGHT: Hurdle fencing surrounding the garden of the Poplar Cottage at the Weald and Downland Museum, Sussex.

have been the white rose, *Rosa x alba*, chosen by Eleanor as her emblem when she married Henry in 1236. Her son, Edmund, is credited with bringing the opposing red rose from France, or Galicia, as its name suggests (*Rosa gallica var. officianalis*).

Royal or not, most gardens of the medieval period were enclosed (the *hortus conclusus*), either by walls or, for less royal domains, wooden fences or hedges. As Chaucer noted in his "Nun's Priest's Tale", "A yerd she hadde, enclosed al aboute; With stikkes, and a drye dych with-oute." Rabbits had made a triumphal re-entry into England with the Normans. Although these particular vegetable predators were still kept in specially constructed warrens and jealously guarded at this time, a fenced garden was needed to keep out a range of other vegetable predators – including human ones. Gardens of apothecaries, wise herb-women, and housewives would also contain the "physic" herbs essential for curing the ills of the day, including pennyroyal for headaches and unwanted pregnancies, sage for sore throats, comfrey for broken bones (hence its common name "knit-bone") and dandelion as a diuretic, also known aptly as "piss-a-bed". Adventurous housewives might include belladonna (deadly nightshade) for eye drops that magnified their pupils and made them shine, whilst incidentally causing deliriums, hallucinations and death if taken incautiously. Mandrake was only planted by those brave enough or clever enough to extract it from the ground without hearing its screams, which were said to send the unfortunate gardener mad.

A sixteenth-century poem in praise of basil:

> *Fine basil desireth it may be her lot*
> *To grow as the gilliflower, trim in a pot*
> *That ladies and gentles, to whom ye do serve*
> *May help her, as needeth, poor life to preserve*
> Thomas Tusser (c. 1524-80)

Although herbs for physic would have been part of most peasant gardens, more essential were the vegetables that would see the family through the year. Winter and early spring crops were prized, including leeks, onions, rampions, skirrets, peas, beans, leaf beet, parsley and the coleworts (a type of non-heading brassica) that were the stalwarts of the peasant diet. So ubiquitous and prized were the worts that the term wortyard was often used to describe the peasant garden before the Conquest. At the Weald and Downland Museum in Singleton (Sussex) several medieval peasant gardens have been recreated, with typical hurdle fences, herb patches and rows of leeks, rampions and skirrets.

As the the climate warmed, new plants arrived on our shores to stay, collected by monks as they moved between monasteries, soldiers coming back from the crusades and wars, and even pilgrims on their wanderings. Vineyards spread across the country in the early fourteenth century. The peach had arrived from China in the thirteenth century, and supposedly caused the death of King John in 1216. Although as he died in October, it seems unlikely that he perished from a surfeit of the tender fruits, despite the claims of his chronicler.

The year 1345 saw the first record of the Worshipful Company of Gardeners in the records of the City Corporation. In 1605, an official Royal Charter lists the operations controlled by the company as:

> *The trade, crafte or misterie of gardening, planting, grafting, setting, sowing, cutting, arboring, rocking, mounting, covering, fencing and removing of plants, herbes, seedes, fruites, trees, stocks, setts, and of contryving the conveyances to the same belonging ...*

MY GARDEN

A garden is a lovesome thing,
God wot!
Rose plot,
Fringed pool,
Ferned grot —
The veriest school
Of peace; and yet the fool
Contends that God is not —
Not God! In gardens! When the
eve is cool?
Nay, but I have a sign;
'Tis very sure God walks in mine.

Thomas Edward Brown (1830–97)

A DESCRIPTION OF THE GARDENS AT HAMPTON COURT

My gardens sweet, enclosed
with walls strong,
Embanked with benches to sytt
and take my rest
The Knotts so enknotted it
cannot be exprest,
With arbours and alys so
pleasant and so dulce,
The pestylent ayers with flavors
to repulse.

*George Cavendish on his Master
Thomas Wolsey's gardens at Hampton
Court before Wolsey "gifted" them to
the king in 1525*

BELOW: The gardens at Kenilworth created by Robert Dudley, Earl of Leicester to impress Elizabeth I. The bear and ragged staff were Dudley's heraldic symbols. The gardens have been recently recreated by English Heritage, giving an insight into what it was like to walk through a Tudor garden.

The Tudor court embraced gardening with enthusiasm. Henry VIII created lavish and colourful gardens at his numerous palaces, including most famously Whitehall, Nonsuch and Hampton Court. At Hampton Court and Whitehall the gardens incorporated painted, striped poles topped with carved heraldic creatures resplendent in gold, green and red – the Tudor colours. At Hampton Court alone there were 159 of these beasts. This bestiary signalled Henry's status and, unlike most garden fashions, appears never to have trickled lower down the social hierarchy. More stripes decorated rails that ran along the edges of the painted raised beds, themselves colourful with the popular flowers of the period such as clove pinks, carnations, lilies, marigolds and "white flowered strawberries". Clove pinks, or gilliflowers, were prized for their scent as well as colours, and were known as "sops in wine" by the Tudors, from their habit of soaking the flowers in wine or beer. Henry VIII may even have had the latest horticultural arrival, then called "broad calf's snout" but better known to later generations as snapdragon or antirrhinum. Walking into the gardens at Hampton Court was a breathtaking sight. Colour and pattern were everywhere, with herbs being used to create chequerboards and knots in the manner of embroidery. Above all this towered the banqueting houses, the largest and most splendid set high on a grass mount and topped with a glittering crown on its onion-dome roof. Three storeys in height, this great "arbour" was rich in glass, a most precious commodity in this period. The King's beasts appeared again in his Pond Garden, a small sunken area which still survives today, although without the menagerie. A description of 1599 tells us that, by then, the gardens also included "all manner of shapes, men and women, half men and half horse, sirens, serving maids with baskets, French lilies and delicate crenellations all round made from dry twigs bound together and the aforesaid ever-green quick-set shrubs, or entirely of rosemary, all true to life and so cleverly and amusingly interwoven, mingled and grown together, trimmed and arranged picture-wise that their equal would be difficult to find". Twenty sundials were also scattered through this astounding garden triumphing the latest developments in science, architecture and gardening.

Although Henry had almost limitless money and power to create gardens, he could not actually be a garden, a device which his daughter Elizabeth came very close to achieving. Poetry, masques and plays celebrated Elizabeth in her role as springtime personified, the Empress of Flowers, the Goddess Flora. Roses, lilies and violets were displaced by her beauty and, in the words of the poet John Davies, "Grene garlands never wasting, In her shall last our State's fair spring, Now and forever flourishing, As long as Heaven is lasting." Elizabeth was too financially adroit to spend money on horticulture and instead left her courtiers to create vast new gardens full of thinly disguised praise to their queen in the guise of the English rose, the honeysuckle or statues of Venus. The most famous of these was the garden at Kenilworth Castle, where Robert Dudley, Earl of Leicester, made his failed bid for the hand of the Queen.

Enthroned as the floral queen, Elizabeth inspired the nation and plants flocked in from the newly discovered Americas. Passionflowers arrived from North America in 1568, followed by French marigolds from Mexico (1572), sunflowers and nasturtiums. Potatoes arrived on these shores for the first time, if not at first into people's kitchens, while the tomato, or love-apple as it was commonly known, appeared in 1597. Both were widely regarded as poisonous, sensibly perhaps as both belong to the Solanum family which also includes deadly nightshade. John Gerard, author of *A Generall Historie of Plantes*, better known now as "Gerard's Herbal", was one of the first people in the country to grow love-apples in his garden. He described them in his herbal as yielding "very little nourishment to the body and the same naught and corrupt". Gerard had over 1,000 different plants in his garden, including such rarities as the yucca, persimmon, a Judas tree and a white mulberry tree. The yucca did not flower for Gerard and the first time its magnificent creamy spikes were seen in England was in the Essex garden of another plant collector, William Coys, in 1604. They caused a sensation and Coys was petrified that the local populace would ransack his garden

Gerard was not a garden writer, and his book concentrates on the uses of plants rather than their decorative qualities. However, the sixteenth century had seen the first ever books on "how to garden". The first, by Thomas Hill, gloried in the title *A Briefe and Pleasant Treatyse, Teaching how to Dress, Sow and Set a Garden*. Published in 1563, it was re-issued in 1577 under the rather snappier title *The Gardener's Labyrinth* (labyrinth meaning a place where many things might be discovered). Hill introduced his readers not only to plants and designs but also to the tools and techniques they might need to use. His illustrations give us the first real insight into gardens owned not by the aristocracy or royalty but by the middling classes. Gardeners are shown using watering pumps to shoot sprays of water over patterns of raised beds, while others weed, cut and graft. Hill includes instructions for setting out knots and patterns, for laying hedges and choosing manure. He also gives his readers this rather unlikely but charmingly naïve hint: "That many savours and tastes may be felte in one herb: take first of the lettuce two or three seeds, of the endive so many,

ABOVE: John Gerard (1545–1611/12) was a gardener, plant collector and writer. He supervised the gardens of William Cecil, Lord Burghley in London as well as having his own gardens at Holborn where he collected rare and unusual plants. The plant he is holding is the first known image of a potato flower.

BELOW: In this image from Thomas Hill's *The Gardener's Labyrinth* men are preparing the soil in raised beds. Against a wall is a shady bower used for playing bowls.

‡ 12 *Tulipa flore albo oris dilute rubentibus.*
The white Tulip with light red edges.
‡ 13 *Tulipa flore pallido.* The ftraw-coloured Tulip.
‡ 14 *Tulipa flammea ftrijs flaveſcentibus.*
The flame coloured Tulip with yellowiſh ftreakes.

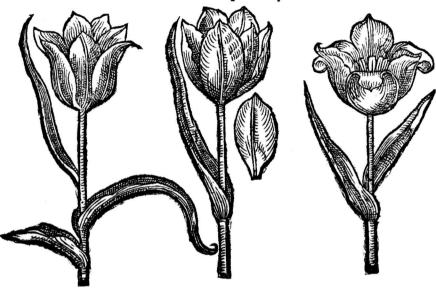

RIGHT: Gerard included the recently introduced tulip in his herbal, noting the various colours and listing 14 types. Thomas Hill called tulips "very beautiful flowers" but noted that they had no scent. One Thomas Fuller, on the other hand, described them as "a well complexioned stink, an ill favour wrapped up in pleasant colours", and expressed his disgust that the plant had no Greek or Latin name. In seventeenth-century gardens, tulips were usually planted in rows, one behind another, like soldiers on parade.

BELOW: John Tradescant the Elder (1570–1638), perhaps the first real plant collector, and his son, also called John.

BELOW: William Lawson's vision of a new orchard and garden in his book of that name published in 1618.

of the smallage, the lyke, of the Basil, the Leek and the Parsley. Put altogether into a hole and there will spring up a plant having so many savours or tastes."

Books lead us onwards as John Parkinson's *Paradisi in Sole, Paradisus Terrestris* of 1629, dedicated to Queen Henrietta Maria, expanded upon Gerard's Herbal, providing illustrations of over 800 plants and descriptions of a thousand. He, too, grew plants imported from round the world in his London gardens, first in Long Acre and then Lambeth. Lambeth is of course rich in its gardening connections, having housed not only Parkinson but also the John Tradescants, Elder and Younger. Parkinson knew Tradescant the Elder well, calling him "my very good friend", and the two must have discussed the new discoveries made by Tradescant, who travelled to Russia, the Levant and Algiers as well as Europe, before becoming the royal gardener. His son continued the search, travelling to the new colonies of America and bringing back with him the tulip tree and magnolias. Both were buried in the grounds of St-Mary-at-Lambeth church, now the Garden Museum, and their tomb stands within the museum gardens. The rare and unusual objects they collected on their travels formed the basis of the Ashmolean Museum in Oxford. John Evelyn completes this circle of horticulturalists – although young at the time, he and the Tradescants had mutual friends in Paris. His own fame came later in the century with the publication of his book *Sylva*, on trees, and his much larger, never-completed, work on the design of gardens and parks. Evelyn also recorded for posterity instructions to his gardener at his own home of Sayes Court (Deptford), including the note that in May he should "Cleanse vines of exuberant Branches and Tendrels".

A GARDEN IS A LOVESOME THING

For most of our nation of gardeners in the sixteenth and seventeenth centuries, tulips and magnolia trees were a distant dream, and even knots were a refinement they had little time for. When they gardened, as they increasingly did, they gardened with an eye to their stomachs. Writing in 1659, the agriculturalist and scientist Samuel Hartlib comments that about 50 years ago "gardening began to creep into England, into Sandwich and Surrey, Fulham and other places. Some old men in Surrey where it flourisheth very much at present, report that they knew the first gardeners that came into those parts to plant cabbages, colleflowers and to sow turneps and carrots and parsnips, and raith-rape peas, all which at that time were great rarities, we having few or none in England but what came from Holland and Flanders."

War and upheaval are not kind to grand gardens and many will have treasured their cabbages and cauliflowers rather than their grand parterres, as the English Civil War overran their estates. But when the monarchy was restored in 1660, courtiers returning from exile on the Continent brought with them ideas for designs of such magnificence that they were to challenge Nature herself. Laid out in an infinity of parterres, with avenues and *allées* that stretched to the horizon and beyond, gardens such as Longleat, Badminton, Chatsworth and the re-designed Hampton Court marked out man's triumph across the land. Flowers were banished to a thin ribbon of colour around vast lawns cut into scroll-work designs and crossed by sand paths. Clipped hedges and topiary abounded and everywhere, in the words of the essayist Joseph Addison, "Our Trees rise in Cones, Globes and Pyramids we see the marks of the Scissars upon every Plant and Bush".

Fashion is a fickle mistress, and soon nature re-entered the garden, smothering the parterres with sweeping lawns and smoothly contouring the once carefully constructed terraces. Leading the way into the landscape was one William Kent, born in Bridlington, trained in Italy and nicknamed "Kentissimo". Horace Walpole, who wrote his *The History of the Modern Taste in Gardening* in the mid-eighteenth century, noted that Kent "leaped the fence, and saw that all nature was a garden". In fact what Kent leapt, or rather inserted for others to leap, was the ha-ha or sunken ditch, which allowed uninterrupted views between the garden and the park. Where Kent led, others followed, although in hindsight Walpole's summing up of Lancelot "Capability" Brown as successor to the brilliant Kent and "a very able master" lacked the enthusiasm now reserved for this most famous landscape designer. Brown it was who was to transform literally thousands of acres of the English landscape into... the English landscape. Nicknamed "Capability" from his habit of pronouncing that a client's estate had great

BELOW: Patterns for knot gardens fiilled early gardening books. Here are some quite complex suggestions in William Lawson's *The Country House-wives Garden* (1617/18). In his 1625 "Essay on Gardens", Sir Francis Bacon dismissively wrote that "as far as the making of knots or figures with diverse coloured earths, they be but toys; you may see as good sights many times in tarts."

BOTTOM: Tools useful for gardeners and florists from the 1706 edition of *Le Jardinier Solitaire* by Gentil.

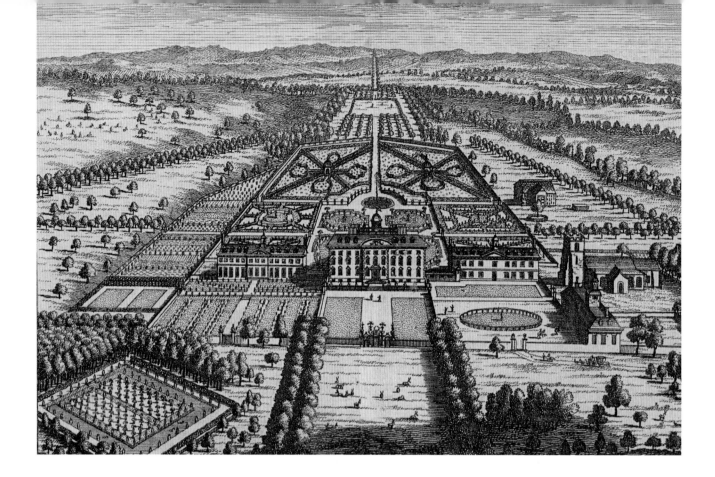

"capabilities" for improvement, Brown took the formal landscapes with their clipped topiary, straight canals, terraces and endless avenues and returned then to nature – so cleverly in fact that Dame Nature herself was said, by the contemporary poet Whitehead, to regret that future generations would not be able to distinguish her work from his. How right she was! Brown's work was so widespread (he "improved" over 150 estates in the terminology of the time) and his influence so ubiquitous that when asked whether he would work in Ireland,

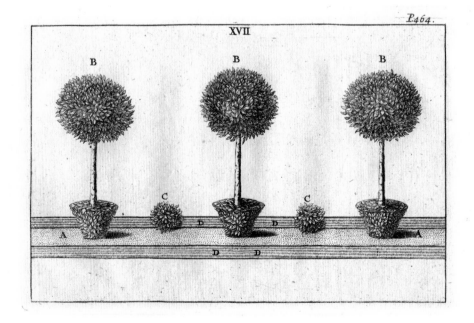

TOP: The gardens at Wimpole Hall, Cambridgeshire stretched to infinity in keeping with late-seventeenth- and early-eighteenth-century fashion.

ABOVE: Pineapples became status symbols of the kitchen garden in the eighteenth century. If your gardener was not skilled enough to grow one, they could be rented by the day to decorate the dinner table, but had to be returned whole!

RIGHT: "The Mark of the Scissars" was everywhere. This illustration comes from one of several French gardening texts translated into English as the fashion for formality swept England.

A GARDEN IS A LOVESOME THING

he replied he had "not yet finished England"; another eminent member of the aristocracy expressed the wish to die before Brown so that he might "see Heaven before it was 'improved'"!

Brown died in 1783, leaving the way open for the man who was to cross the divide between the polite landscapes of the eighteenth century and the gardenesque style of the Regency and early Victorians. Humphry Repton, much to his own regret, was never able to rival the scale of work carried out by Brown. The Napoleonic Wars (1799–1815) and the agricultural depression that followed meant that Repton's clientele was composed of the merchant classes rather than the aristocracy. If Kent had seen that all nature was a garden, Repton created a garden from that nature, and put a fence around it. Fences, after all, make good neighbours, and the "polite society" of Jane Austen depended on good relations with your neighbours – you might even marry them! Repton receives a name-check from Austen in *Mansfield Park*, as available to hire by the day for five guineas and guaranteed to "give as much beauty as he can" for the money. Surely even a nation of gardeners could not ask for more?

ABOVE: The return of flowers to the garden was a hallmark of the Regency garden. Bedding displays were often of varied heights with much earth on show around the individual plants. The rustic seat and arbour, glasshouse and "plant theatre" portrayed here in Charles Mcintosh's *The Practical Gardener* (1828 edition) were all popular features.

LEFT: Humphry Repton's own garden at Hare Street typified his later designs which would lead into Victorian garden fashion.

2

What the Victorians Dug for Us: Innovation and Inspiration

PREVIOUS PAGE: A lean-to glasshouse has been tacked on to the side of this modest detached villa house, photographed in the 1870s, while the central feature is inspired by similar ones at the Great Exhibiition of 1851. In modern terms this garden would be "upwardly mobile"!

ABOVE: Aspirational gardeners were inspired by planting designs such as this in the grounds of the Royal Horticultural Society c.1870.

OPPOSITE BELOW: Carpet bedding in Hesketh Park, Southport. The postcard dates from 1910, by which time bedding like this was unfashionable in private gardens and had become largely confined to public parks.

The ascent to the British throne of Queen Victoria in 1837 ushered in a period of industrial and scientific progress across the nation, and in the nation's gardens. From glasshouses to lawnmowers, carpet bedding to fern collecting, the Victorian garden was vibrant with innovation and opportunity. New books and periodicals filled the shelves of anxious amateur gardeners, and suburban villa gardens spilled over with exotic plants newly discovered in the Americas and South Africa. As the middle classes colonized suburbia, they brought the consumer society with them. Using the railways to deliver seeds and summerhouses, they embellished and adorned their gardens under the instructions of gardening heroes such as John Claudius Loudon (author of the *Suburban Gardener and Villa Companion*, 1838) and Shirley Hibberd, the suburban classes' guide to taste in the garden. Although the grand houses also reached a gardening peak during this period, with swathes of brightly coloured annual bedding vying with statuesque palms and Italianate terraces, it was the amateur gardener who held sway over the nation's gardens, equipped with a range of tools which satisfied the Victorians' delight in the multi-functional, and with an array of periodicals, advertisements and seed packets.

A circle of bedding plants set in the lawn, endless scarlet geraniums and a shady shrubbery sums up many people's image of a Victorian garden, and

WHAT THE VICTORIANS DUG FOR US: INNOVATION AND INSPIRATION

for small suburban gardens these were indeed the essentials. Larger gardens might add to this a rose garden, with pillar supports and rope swags, an area of rock-work (either with ferns or alpines), a small lily pond and brightly planted borders using the fashionable "ribbon bedding" in lines of colour. A central fountain graced the most aspirational of gardens, while a glasshouse was essential to guarantee a constant supply of tender annual bedding plants raised from seed. Cut into the lawn, bedding shapes and planting became more and more complex from the 1840s onwards. Circles, ovals and kidney shapes were joined by stars, "tadpoles", crescents and even butterflies and hearts. Raising up the centres of the beds increased the variety of designs, with raised "pincushions", mounds and geranium pyramids.

The most popular of plants were the brightly coloured imports from the hotter climes of South America and South Africa: heliotrope from Peru, also known as cherry pie from its almost overpoweringly sweet smell; the bright yellow calceolaria from the Andes and Mexico; verbenas, petunias and begonias completing the riot of colour. From South Africa, lobelias and gazanias joined the pelargoniums which had arrived in the eighteenth century and had patiently awaited their moment in garden fashion. Although it was not until 1844 that the first scarlet geranium burst upon the scene – a dwarf variety named Tom Thumb – promptly followed by all shades of pinks, salmons and mauves. Mostly lost to us today, these popular varieties of geranium included Mrs Pollock, West Brighton Gem, Egyptian Queen, Mrs Henry Cox, Black Vesuvius, Crystal Palace, Mangles's Variegated (named after the nurseryman Mangles) and the rather ominously named Freak of Nature, another variegated variety.

Carpet bedding relied on all the plants in the bed being at the same (low) height to produce the idea of a carpet. Its peak of popularity in private gardens was over by the 1880s, although it continued in public parks well into the

PANSY, MIXED

ABOVE: Pansies could be used to bring late summer and autumn colour to bedding schemes.

VILLA GARDENS

"A villa garden, as a rule, contains just enough space to be within the means of the owner or occupier to keep in order, and it happens more often than not that he does so even to a lavish extent. In doing so he is only acting in perfect harmony with the natural order of things, and everyone that has the means should certainly strive to have not only his house but his garden beautiful also."
Amateur Gardening, 1888

CARPET GARDEN HESKETH PARK, SOUTHPORT.

BELOW: The front garden of the garden writer Shirley Hibberd, demonstrating the use of tulips in a colourful seasonal planting scheme. Hibberd had a "typical" suburban villa garden in Stoke Newington, north London.

twentieth century. Plants that were ideal for this style included *Ajuga reptans*, arabis, dwarf creeping mint, and of course the lower-growing sedums and sempervivums. Foliage plants such as coleus and euonymus might be included, whilst taller palms or drachaenas would, in the words of *The Amateur's Flower Garden* (1901 edition), "relieve the flatness". In this riot of colour, bulbs and tuberous flowers also had their place, with tulips, lilies, gladioli and alstroemeria occupying pride of place and chinadoxa taking their spot in the rockery garden.

Seeds for bedding plants, along with other flowers and vegetables, could be sent easily and cheaply using the new postal and railway services, or purchased directly from seed merchants. Sutton's and Carters' Seeds were both founded in 1806, although Sutton did not branch out into flowers and vegetable seeds until 1837, having originated as corn merchants. Carters' were recommended for their zinnias by Elizabeth Watts in her book *Modern Practical Gardening*

WHAT THE VICTORIANS DUG FOR US: INNOVATION AND INSPIRATION

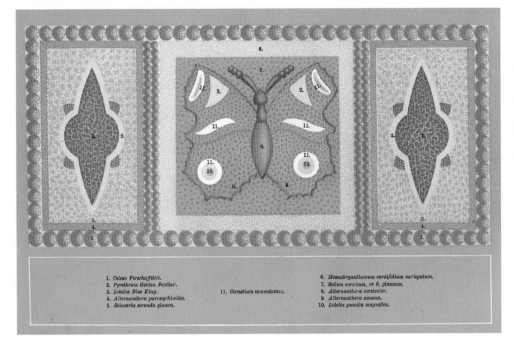

LEFT: For the ambitious amateur, Thompson's *The Gardener's Assistant* set high standards with a series of complex shapes and patterns in the "plant by numbers" design ideas. The designs were said to "represent some of the best examples in the London parks in 1875".

(published in 1865). By the end of Victoria's reign in 1837, you could also buy seeds from Barr's, Dick Radcliffe and Ryder & Sons, amongst others.

For the Victorian gardener and garden writer, gardening was so much more than just flowers and bedding. As Shirley Hibberd, author of *Rustic Adornments of Homes of Taste*, proclaimed:

> *The pleasures of the garden … the culture of choice plants in the greenhouse and the window, seem to me much more remunerative, both intellectually and morally, than even the study of the higher departments of life, because they keep us nearer to nature and compel us to be students of the great out-door world, whence our noblest inspirations and most humanizing teachings are drawn.*

Hibberd was a teetotal vegetarian and may have taken his moralistic values rather further than most Victorian gardeners were prepared to go. Yet sentimentality, a taste for the rustic and memories of the "happy cottage garden" which the families of so many urban dwellers had left only two or three generations before, were all influences on the popularity of gardening. In a period when the influx of new plants from around the world highlighted – as most people believed – the bounteous and inventive nature of God, acquiring plants could almost be seen as a form of worship. In fact, many of the famous gardeners of the eighteenth and nineteenth centuries were clergymen. Men like the Reverend Gilbert White of Selborne (1720–93), Samuel Reynolds Hole (1819–1904), Dean of Rochester, garden writer and rose lover, or Henry Nicholson Ellacombe, Canon of Bristol, Vicar of Bitten and author of *In a Gloucestershire Garden*. Canon Ellacombe even found time to write a gardening column in the *Guardian*. Some of his gardening axioms do sound as much like sermons as gardening advice.

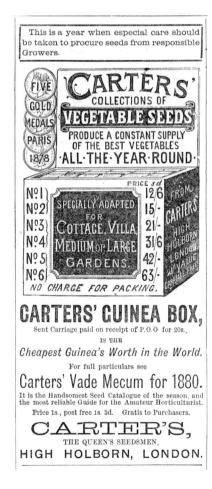

ABOVE: By the end of the nineteenth century Carters' were one of the most popular seed suppliers, with a range to suit every pocket.

ABOVE: The family that gardened together stayed together! At least that was what the Victorians thought. Shared family values, healthy living and "clean minds" were all part of the fashion for gardening.

The fair-weather gardener, who will do nothing except when wind and weather and everything else are favourable, is never a master of his craft. Gardening, above all other crafts, is a matter of faith, grounded, however (if on nothing better); on his experience that somehow or other seasons go on in their right course, and bring their right results. No doubt bad seasons are a trial of his faith; it is grievous to lose the fruits of much labour by a frosty winter or a droughty summer, but, after all, frost and drought are necessities for which, in all his calculations, he must leave an ample margin; but even in the extreme cases, when the margin is past, the gardener's occupation is not gone.

For most amateur gardeners, however, the religious side of gardening was bound up with the ideal of family values, hard work and thrift, the latter sitting rather oddly with the opportunities for consumerism provided by the new fashion for gardening by mail order. Shirley Hibberd proclaimed that there had never been a gardener who was a murderer, although notably he gave no evidence to back up his claim that horticulture placated the homicidal. The anonymous "Rosa" who wrote a column entitled "My Flowers" each week in *The Cottage Gardener* also leaned heavily on religious homilies. In October 1848, she mused that:

I love to ask my little [flower] charges how they do after the dewy hours of the night ... the shining drops tremble and sparkle so prettily in their tiny cups, and they seem so fully to enjoy their repast that it makes me almost wish that I could live upon dewdrops too.

Then in August the following year she instructed her readers to:

Let the blooming creepers round our cottage porch instruct us, and lead us to twine our hopes and affections around "those things that are above and Him whose strength is made perfect in our weakness".

ABOVE: This glass cucumber straightener was one of many Victorian gardening accoutrements. These straighteners were supposedly invented by George Stephenson of "Rocket" fame.

LEFT: One of many publications by Jane Loudon, wife of the astoundingly productive John Claudius Loudon.

Rosa's column was axed the following year, suggesting that she had overdone the sentimentality, even for Victorian tastes.

With the increased interest in gardening, and the reduction and eventual abolition of the paper tax (in 1836 and 1855), came the first flood of gardening periodicals. During the eighteenth century, periodicals had been aimed at the botanist, flower fancier (florist) or collector, but during the Victorian period a host of other titles could be delivered to the door by the new cheap postal service. The most popular for the amateur gardener were *Amateur Gardening*, the *Gardener's Magazine* (edited by John Loudon himself), the *Cottage Gardener*, and Shirley Hibberd's *The Floral World and Garden Guide*. Later in the century, these were joined by *Cottage Gardening* and *Gardening Illustrated*. Other periodicals such as the *Floral Magazine*, the *Floricultural Cabinet* or the *Florist's Journal* catered for those whose interest lay in the plants rather than gardens. Many of the weeklies were priced at one or two pennies a week, although the florists' magazines could cost as much as four shillings a copy.

The Victorians adored invention and ingenuity, and garden tools were favourite objects for innovation. The gardening periodicals of the period were full of advertisements for items that promised to revolutionize gardening, from the painful-sounding sphincter hose and garden syringes to the averruncator (a pruner for large shrubs, variously spelt) and cucumber straightener. The

ABOVE: These multiple trimmers were heavy, awkward, and necessitated constant sharpening and oiling, but inventions fascinated the Victorians.

LEFT: Garden periodicals were typically comprised of dense small type, with sparse illustrations. But as the nineteenth century wore on, colour pages became more frequent. These copies of *Amateur Gardening* have been carefully bound.

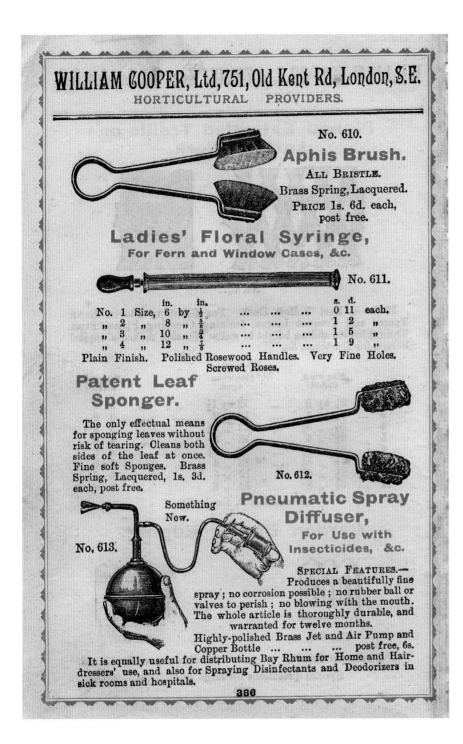

LEFT: Sponges were used to wash the leaves of plants that struggled to survive in the soot-laden atmosphere both indoors and out.

basic needs of the gardener remained very much the same as they had been for centuries: in 1840, Mrs Louisa Johnson recommended that the economical lady gardener should purchase a light spade, two rakes, a light garden fork, a watering pot, a hoe, two trowels of different sizes and shapes, a pair of hedge shears, a pruning knife and a "stout deep basket" (for the weeds). Beyond this list, she states, "all else is superfluous and will serve only to decorate the wall of your tool house," although she was prepared to allow the "avroncater" as an admirable instrument, albeit rather too expensive for her readers. Regardless

BELOW: The patented "Hydronette" relied on manually pumping pressure in a similar way to the modern "killaspray". It revolutionized watering and washing down plants, although the jet of water shown in this advertisement would knock down most plants!

of Mrs Johnson's sound advice, Victorian gardeners were only too eager to surround themselves with the superfluous, if the numerous advertisements are anything to go by. Particularly popular were tools that either combined two purposes or were in some way disguised. For example, a basket for weeds that incorporated a long-handled weeder in its handle or a walking stick with a pruning saw inside it or a short weed-digger on the end. The word "patented" in an advertisement brought a shiver of excitement to Victorians, who held that newly invented tools and machines should be regarded as an advancement in civilization – and of course in gardening.

The foremost garden innovation of the Victorian period was the lawnmower. Actually invented by Edwin Budding in 1827 (patented in 1830), the lawnmower had a slow start in life. Traditionally, lawns were cut with scythes, and a skilled hand with a scythe was looked on with as much pride as we now regard the immaculately striped lawn. In order to obtain the required short cut, a scythe would be adjusted in length for the height of the man using it, although it was still up to him to ensure the blade was used at a perfect horizontal to the ground. In large gardens, teams of scythers

THE HYDRONETTE.
(IMPROVED TREBLE TUBE.)

would go out before dawn, whilst the dew was still on the grass, and cut it to a velvet perfection. In his popular 1879 work *A Year in a Lancashire Garden* Henry Bright rejoiced in the sound of the "strong sharp sweep of the scythe as it whistles through the falling grass, or the shrill murmur of the blade on the whetstone; and in spite of mowing machines, at times one hears the old sound still."

At first, Budding envisaged his new lawn-mowing machine would appeal to those with areas of shady gardens, where the grass did not grow dense enough for the scythe, or for country gentlemen who, he said, "may find, in using the machine themselves, an amusing, useful and healthy exercise". But it was the economy of the machine, rather than any health-giving properties, which

THE AUTOMATON LAWN MOWER.

DESIGNED & MANUFACTURED BY
RANSOMES, SIMS & HEAD,
ORWELL WORKS, IPSWICH.

RANSOMES, SIMS & HEAD, have had great experience in the manufacture of Lawn Mowers, extending over a period of thirty years. R. S. & H. brought out their Automaton Lawn Mowers in 1867, from entirely new designs and patterns, embodying the Latest Improvements, and from the universal approbation they have met with, R. S. & H. can with the greatest confidence recommend them to their friends.

The best and simplest plan of communicating motion to the knives is adopted, viz., by accurate MACHINE MADE GEARING, which is far superior to chains and other methods; as whilst almost noiseless, it is not liable to get out of order.

The CUTTING-BARRELS are fitted with the best steel knives, and the pivots are of hardened steel, working in hard steel cones, so that these important parts will last several seasons without perceptible wear.

These machines leave no ribs in the grass, but a beautiful flat uniform surface is obtained, very far superior to any work that can be done with a scythe, and at a much less cost.

THEY ARE EXTREMELY SIMPLE, VERY DURABLE, LIGHT IN DRAUGHT,
AND NOT LIABLE TO GET OUT OF ORDER.

MORE THAN 4,000 AUTOMATON LAWN MOWERS
have been sold since their introduction in 1867, and
ARE GIVING THE GREATEST SATISFACTION.
A few Testimonials are given on the other side.

THE PRICES ARE AS UNDER:
Including Free Delivery to the Principal Railway Stations and Shipping Ports in England.

8 inch, suitable for very small Lawns	£2 15 0	16 inch, to be used by a Man .	. £6 10 0
10 inch } suitable for a Lady or Lad	3 10 0	18 inch, to be used by a Man	. 7 10 0
12 inch	4 10 0	20 inch, to be used by a Man and Boy	8 0 0
14 inch, to be used by a Lad . .	5 10 0		

Packing Cases, 5s. extra. These Cases are most convenient for keeping the Machines in during the Winter.

A New Horse-Power Machine, with draft-bar complete, 36 inch, suitable for
a Horse or Pony . . . £24.

RANSOMES, SIMS & HEAD, guarantee these Machines to perform their work perfectly, and if not approved of, they may be returned, carriage paid, within a month.

See description of NEWLY DESIGNED GARDEN ROLLERS on the other side.

ENTERED AT STATIONERS' HALL

LEFT: This 1868 advertisement for a lawnmower is rare. It dates from the first years of lawnmower manufacture and the brief period of Ransomes, Sims & Head, the company that was eventually to become Ransomes. By the early twentieth century Ransomes was one of the leading lawnmower manufacturers and producers of the first commercially available petrol-driven lawnmower. Note the grass box.

BELOW: Horses and ponies would wear these bootees whilst mowing to prevent marks on the turf.

ensured its eventual success. Few middle-class householders were proficient scythers and so, as lawns became an essential feature of the fashionable garden, it was necessary either to employ a scyther or invest in a mower. In the shorter term the scyther was cheaper (hired by the day once a week or a fortnight) – but in the longer term the mower won out.

Soon lawnmowers were available in all sizes and shapes, and even with different motive powers: one-man lawnmowers; two-man mowers (one pushing and one pulling); mowers pulled by ponies or horses (for the larger lawn only!); lawnmowers for ladies and children; and even steam-driven lawnmowers by the end of the century. The addition of grass boxes did away with the need for a small boy with a broom to clear up the cuttings. The grass box was initially just a flat tray, with a tendency for the grass to fall off the other end, but by the 1860s it had assumed its present shape and become an excellent spot for the manufacturer's name. Other accoutrements included pony shoes, leather bootees which fitted over a pony's hooves and allowed them to pull a lawnmower without cutting up the precious turf. Croquet, first played in England in the 1850s but at the height of popularity by the 1870s, added to the pressure to have a perfect lawn, followed by the growing vogue for lawn tennis in the 1890s.

After a lawnmower, a glasshouse was the next "must have" for the Victorian amateur gardener. Originally called "stoves" (as they were heated by coal stoves) or greenhouses (as they kept your plants green over winter), protective houses used for tender plants or for extending cropping seasons had been popular in larger gardens from the eighteenth century. However, with the repeal of the glass tax in 1845, and the repeal of the brick tax in 1850, glasshouses of all kinds came within the financial reach of the amateur. Inspired by London's Crystal Palace and the Great Exhibition of 1851, glasshouses came in all shapes and sizes, although for the economically minded the lean-to was the most economical. Joseph Paxton, head gardener at Chatsworth in Derbyshire and designer of the Crystal Palace, had no need for such economies. His employer, the Duke of Devonshire, gave him an almost unlimited budget to construct the Great Stove at Chatsworth, which housed his vast collection of exotics. The Great Stove was so large that when Queen Victoria and Prince Albert visited in 1843, they were able to drive through it

ADIE'S LAWN EDGE CLIPPER.

Cash Price, 10/- each.
Carriage Paid with other Goods amounting to 40/- value.

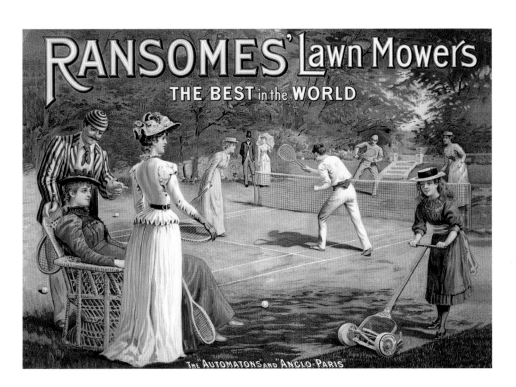

THE "AUTOMATONS" AND "ANGLO-PARIS"

ABOVE: The lawnmover inspired other offshoots in the garden, including this lawn edger driven by a wheel. It is difficult to believe that it gave a neat edge on any but the most level surface.

LEFT: Garden games such as lawn tennis were a boost for the lawnmower industry. Lawn tennis became extremely popular from the 1890s onwards.

THE EXTERIOR, FROM THE ITALIAN TERRACE.

ABOVE: The "Great Stove" at Chatsworth was designed by the head gardener, Joseph Paxton, who later designed the Crystal Palace for the 1851 Great Exhibition and oversaw its subsequent move to Sydenham. Both the Crystal Palace and the Great Stove employed new technologies in glass and metalwork.

in a coach, their way lit by 14,000 candles. When Charles Darwin visited this miniature floral world in 1845, he wrote that he was "transported with delight ... The water part is more wonderfully like tropical nature than I would have thought possible. Art beats nature altogether there."

For the enthusiastic amateur gardener, one glasshouse would not be enough, and even modest gardens might sprout a cucumber house, a vinery, a fernery, a "plant house" (for pots that would be later placed indoors or on terraces) and even an orchid house. Each of these was made with a slightly different design to allow for the plants' preferences for sun or shade, humidity or fresh air, whether the plants rooted in pots or in the ground, cool or hot, and of course, whether they were expensive or cheap. As manufacturing techniques improved, glass could be made in increasingly large panes, while the innovation of wrought-

AZALEA.
Reine Marie Henrietta.

iron in glasshousing meant that different shapes could also be made, including curved and decorative roofs.

Unsurprisingly, as Victorian glasshouses multiplied so did books on how to use them. The Loudons, as ever, led the way for the middle classes. In 1848, Jane Loudon published the *Ladies' Flower-Garden of Ornamental Greenhouse Plants*, one in a series of Ladies' Flower Garden titles which included volumes on ornamental annuals, perennials and the rather oddly named *Ladies' Flower-Garden of Ornamental Bulbous Plants*. As well as writing about glasshouses, in his compendious *The Suburban Gardener and Villa Companion*, her husband John Claudius Loudon also designed them, introducing refinements such as the "ridge and furrow" roofed glasshouse.

In 1873, Shirley Hibberd brought out his 300-page *The Amateur's*

ABOVE: With the aid of a cool greenhouse, Shirley Hibberd assured his readers that fashionable plants such as this wonderful azalea could be theirs.

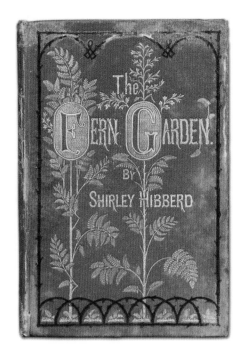

ABOVE: Books on fern collecting and gardening were often exquisitely decorated. This 1872 example dates from the height of the fern craze.

BELOW: Not content with instructing you inside the house, the Beetons offered advice for the outside as well!

Greenhouse and Conservatory, subtitled – with the prolixity for which the Victorians are known – *A Handy Guide to the Construction and Management of Plant-Houses, the Selection, Cultivation and Improvement of Ornamental Greenhouse and Conservatory Plants*. A contemporary reviewer extolled the work, noting that "There seems to be nothing neglected, down to the very crocking of a pot, which, as well as most other particulars, is well illustrated by woodcuts. Select lists of plants suitable for various seasons, circumstances, and purposes are furnished, which, to the inexperienced amateur, must prove of great use."

Alongside the glasshouses for sun-loving plants, special glasshouses were also constructed for shade-loving ferns. The craze for fern collecting and growing was known as "pteridomania" and took off in the 1850s. Whole swathes of the Lake District, the West Country and Wales were denuded of their ferns, which were rolled up in sheets and transported triumphantly by their collectors back to suburban homes. Fern mania was particularly popular with young women, giving them the opportunity to go on fern-hunting expeditions which comprised both men and women. This was rather ironic, as the fern craze had in part originated because ferns were seen as suitably non-sexual plants for female botanic studies! Once home, the ferns needed housing. Fortunately, even the dark and shady gardens of urban London proved suitable for their needs, fuelling their popularity even further. The hardier ferns could be set into rockery collections or brought indoors to struggle with the gas lighting and stifling atmosphere of the Victorian living room.

Having created the perfect garden and grown the perfect plants – preferably flowering or fruiting them a month before their neighbour did – many Victorian amateur gardeners then joined in the competitive challenge of the horticultural or cottage garden show. These had originated in the main as shows for amateur breeders of fancy flowers (or "florist's flowers") such as auriculus, tulips, anemones, carnations and picotees, but there were also specialist gooseberry shows (for the largest gooseberry) and more general horticultural shows. The success of the general show was furthered by the support of the upper classes, who often donated prizes and even entertainment and food in the belief that such shows kept men away from the ale house and busy down the allotment. Shows were divided between the regional or national florists' shows and the local village show – although it was often complained that gardeners from the "big house" would enter the local shows and win all the prizes. In order to overcome this, some shows developed a complex system of rules which meant that professional gardeners might only enter specific classes – even if the plants they entered had been grown in their spare time in their own gardens. Within the general shows, classes such as chrysanthemums or asters attracted intense competition and gained income for the clubs that

LEFT: The annual show was often the highlight of the village year. This prize has been won by a woman.

BELOW: A specialized fern trowel with its storage sleeve. This example dates to c. 1900.

ran them. In 1880, the Chrysanthemum Society of Stoke Newington had 700 members and an income of £850 a year. The garden writer Shirley Hibberd, who lived in Stoke Newington, claimed that the success of the chrysanthemum societies had resulted in a decrease in the number of late-autumn suicides, as members of such societies had their November show to look forward to. He did not, though, go on to mention whether there was subsequently a peak in December suicides amongst those who had failed to obtain prizes.

VILLAGE HORTICULTURAL SHOWS

"Previous to some eight or ten years since, the village alluded to [Etal] was one of the most wicked places that could be found. It was no uncommon sight to see, on leaving the house of God, which was situated on a 'green', a number of the most depraved of men collected round a cock-fight, dog-fight or even man-fight, giving utterance to the most horrid imprecations and blasphemy. Now, some of the men who were once at the head of all descriptions of vice, are the principal exhibitors, and are remarkable for their Christian bearing and industrial [sic] habits. Pieces of ground which then bore nothing but crops of nettles and thistles are now clothed with the gayest beauties of the floral kingdom, or groaning under the loads of the finest vegetables that can possibly be grown. It is astonishing that in such a short space of time such a revolution could take place. The houses which were once dens of poverty and filth are now changed into neat white-washed cottages. The public house is giving way to the reading room, and the cock-fights to the shows. And all this, I believe, to have been caused by the establishment of a horticultural society."

J. L. Middlemiss, gardener to A. Pott Esq, Tunbridge Wells. In 25 October 1848, The Cottage Gardener

3

Sowing the Seed: Gardening for Children

SWISS COTTAGE, OSBORNE
GARDEN TOOLS OF THE ROYAL CHILDREN

H. M. Office of Woo

PREVIOUS PAGE: As Adam dug and Eve
watered – a nineteenth-century slant on
the original story of Eden.

ABOVE: Captured here in the nineteenth
century, the royal gardening tools are still
preserved at Osborne House on the Isle
of Wight.

For as long as gardens have existed, children have been set to work, to water
and weed. Little fingers have picked caterpillars from brassicas and peas
from their pods under the watchful eyes of busy parents. In the medieval and
Tudor periods, children worked in the fields and gardens from the ages of eight
or earlier, guarding precious crops from birds with noisy rattles.

The idea of having special gardens just for children was, however, largely
an invention of the Victorian middle classes. Maria Edgeworth set the scene
in the late eighteenth century with her educational and moral texts urging
parents to introduce their children to the joys of weeding at the age of six or
seven, whilst older children could discover the delights of a spade, a hoe, a rake
and a wheelbarrow. Leading naturally on to an interest in botany and nature
studies, the garden was seen as an ideal way to educate children in everything
from Latin nomenclature to religion. In 1838, the famous garden writer of the
period John Claudius Loudon commented: "What pleasure have not children
in applying their little green watering-pans to plants in pots, or pouring water in
at the roots of favourite flowers in borders?"

Queen Victoria and Prince Albert set the fashion in children's gardens in
the mid-nineteenth century by providing each of their nine children with their
own garden at the royal residence of Osborne House on the Isle of Wight, each
of them equipped with a complete set of tools and wheelbarrows with the royal

SOWING THE SEED: GARDENING FOR CHILDREN

children's initials painted on in gold. They grew fruit, flowers and vegetables on their own individual plots, overlooked by a Swiss cottage and a small thatched summerhouse, where the tools were kept when not in use.

Prince Albert, himself the patron of the Royal Horticultural Society and a keen gardener, encouraged the children by paying them for their produce. Account books were kept of seeds bought and produce sold. This, Albert said, taught them the basics of the market economy as well as the precepts of horticulture, although it seems unlikely that Prince Albert was up to date with the going rate for cabbages. How much of the actual gardening was done by the royal princes and princesses must remain uncertain, as the royal family were only in residence at Osborne during May, July, August and December of each year. In between these times, the plots must either have been very weedy or had the attentions of the more stay-at-home gardeners. Perhaps a series of garden boys looked after the plots while the more regal children were away.

Where royalty led, the rest of the nation followed, and soon small plots of sunflowers, sweet-peas and nasturtiums were being lovingly tended by children in more humble settings, although, as ever, styles in gardens were often dictated by class. In her *Letter from a Little Garden* in 1886, Mrs Horatia Ewing instructed her young readers on the superiority of hardy plants over annual bedding, but cautioned them to disguise their distaste if they found themselves visiting children with less fastidious parents. The anxious young gardeners who read Mrs Ewing's *Mary's Meadow*, serialized in *Aunt Judy's Magazine* in the 1880s, were instructed on topsoil, compost and how to plant borders. The children in the story were inspired by the seventeenth-century book *Paradisi in Sole, Paradisus Terrestris* (by John Parkinson) to create their own "paradise on Earth". Why they needed make their own compost, despite there being frequent references to "the gardener" employed by their parents, was never really explained and Mary's own determination to become a lowly paid "weeding woman" when she grew up was no doubt a flight of fantasy her middle-class parents would have been anxious to dispel as soon as possible.

For most middle-class Victorian and Edwardian children, "gardening" entailed nothing more arduous than watering and weeding, although the weighty galvanized metal watering cans of the period meant that even this was heavy work. As the fashion for children's gardens grew, manufacturers started to make especially small garden tools for the new market. Soon, even children without recourse to

ABOVE: This child's watering can of the 1930s is decorated in Mabel Lucie Atwell style.

BELOW: Wheelbarrows and watering cans were made in special child sizes. Despite the long hair, this is a little boy.

a royal carpenter could not only weed and water, but also dig and even mow the lawn, although Gertrude Jekyll later called these children's tools "wretched tools, badly shaped, badly balanced and generally weakest where they should be strongest". Regardless of their merits as tools, a child with a watering can or wheelbarrow became a popular subject for artists and engravers during the Victorian and Edwardian periods and even into the 1950s. Again it was Queen Victoria who started the fashion, being pictured in 1828 – when she was still Princess Victoria – watering the flowers at Kensington Palace.

By the end of the nineteenth century gardening had become an established part of the school curriculum and most schools boasted at least a small patch of ground for both flowers and vegetables. As early as 1879, a course of 16 lectures entitled "Town and Window Gardening" was given to pupil teachers and children attending the Leeds board's schools. The need for crops to grow and mature before the school year ended led to an emphasis on quick-growing crops such as radishes, lettuce and carrots. In June 1906, Lucy Latter, a teacher of nature studies and author of *School Gardening for Little Children*, recorded that the climax of the month's gardening endeavours was "a grand feast of radishes shared by many of the children's parents and some friends". Lucy Latter was keen to promote gardening for children as encouraging a quickened power of observation, intelligence and refinement, and noted anxiously that school gardening studies on the Continent were far in advance of those in England.

RIGHT: This child-sized wheelbarrow has been outgrown by its owner.

BELOW: A young Princess Victoria at Kensington Palace c.1828.

Account of Workmen's Time Employed on the Duke of Sutherland's *Gardens* at Lilleshall from *May 12* 1904 to *May 26* 1904 inclusive.

No.	NAME.	Employment.	Days.	Rate.	Amount.	To whom paid.
1	Calt William	Forman	7	3/6	1 4 6	
2	Heardman John	—	5	3/4	1 6 8	
3	Edwards Charles	Journeyman	12	3/8	1 2 0	
4	Worrell Alfred	—	12	3/0	1 4 0	
5	Birch Charles	Groom	12	3/10	1 14 0	
6	Price Awlther	K Gardens	12	3/0	1 16 0	
7	Hasly James	Labourer	11	3/6	1 7 6	
8	Cooper Richard	Labourer	11	3/6	1 7 6	
9	Millington Ben	Labourer	9	3/6	1 2 6	
10	Blest John	Labourer	11	3/6	1 7 6	
11	Plevin Joe	Labourer	12	3/6	1 10 0	
12	Ledham Eustis	Boy	12	1/2	14 0	
13	Hasly Richard	Boy	12	1/2	14 0	
14	Shucker John	—	12	1/0	10 0	
15	Mrs Allen	Cleaning			16 0	
16	Heardman John	Na-Effen			12 0	
					18 2 2	

Germany in particular had school gardens in almost every village. Nature studies, which included gardening, were often taught by a woman and were one of the careers especially recommended to young women in the early 1900s, particularly those with a background in botanical studies or from the new ladies' gardening schools.

If gardening was seen as morally and intellectually uplifting for children of the middle classes in the Victorian and Edwardian periods, it was an essential activity for those of the working classes. Many country boys learnt how to grow fruit and vegetables from their fathers, whilst the girls cultivated flowers and herbs, but those that wanted to go on to work in the large kitchen gardens of the local "big house" would be expected to have taken an interest in school. Until the end of the nineteenth century, the age that children started work was as young as 10 or 12, and even after the school-leaving age was recommended to be raised to 14 in 1918, it was still possible to get a special certificate to start work at 13 if you already had a job lined up. Herbert Watkinson from Chippenham (Suffolk) was

offered a job in the kitchen garden of the local manor house at the age of 13 in the 1930s, and stayed working on the estate until he retired 50 years later. Garden boys, or "pot boys" as they were often known, would earn less than half of the wages of the trainee gardeners and would commonly carry out the more repetitive or menial duties. As well as the inevitable weeding and watering, young boys in country house gardens would wash the pots, help spray chemicals such as nicotine in the glasshouses, and stoke the boilers. Unlike their more leisured counterparts, these young boys would have to use bulky and heavy adult tools.

The Edwardian period saw a flurry of books on gardening for children, increasingly aimed at the children themselves rather than their parents. *The Children's Book of Gardening* by Mrs Sidgwick and Mrs Paynter led children through the the different gardening tasks, explaining along the way the difference between hardy perennials, annuals and bedding plants. Although the high moral tone of earlier works is missing, the authors do still warn their charges that "some people will be very angry with us for advising you to grow anything in lines. Lines are out of fashion, and they certainly have been made to give hideous effects by the ignorant gardener. But we make bold to think that a child who

RIGHT & FAR RIGHT: Myrta Higgins's (1910) book for children encouraged a blaze of colour rather than the subtler delights of love in a mist and roses favoured by the more Arts and Crafts-influenced writers such as Charles Wyatt (far right).

BELOW: This delightful pot of tulips was designed for Queen Mary's dolls' house.

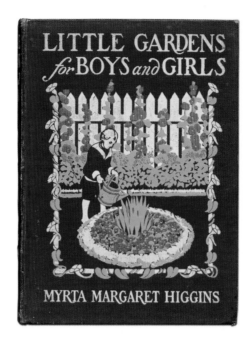

wants a blaze of colour all the summer in its small patch will get what he wants if he grows his garden as contrary Mary did, 'all in a row.'" The blaze of colour was added to with fragrant mignonette, sweet-peas, nasturtium, wallflowers, lilies and roses. These simple plants were also popular with Myrta Margaret Higgins, who wrote *Little Gardens for Boys and Girls* (1910), which had a perfectly circular bed of bright red annuals on its front cover.

The authors of *The Children's Book of Gardening* did not give much instruction on fruit and vegetable gardening as "a child is not likely to want his little garden to be a vegetable garden", but they did give advice on radishes, carrots, lettuce and gooseberry and currant bushes. Gooseberry bushes were often associated with children even in grown-ups' cottage gardens. In *Cottage Gardening: A Practical Manual* (1896) it was recommended that families with children should plant as many as two dozen gooseberry bushes, as children devoured the fruits! In between devouring gooseberries, Edwardian children were instructed in such risky tasks as spreading lime and soot (against slugs), mixing liquid manure, taking cuttings with a sharp knife and spraying liquid paraffin mix against aphids. That any young gardeners grew to adulthood seems almost miraculous.

Spotting a gap in the market, the seed merchants Sutton's sold specific collections of flower seeds suitable for children's gardens. The first collection (price 2s 6d in 1909) contained 12 varieties of annuals including nigella, sweet pea, mignonette, malope, antirrhinum, nasturtium, clarkia, shirley poppy, wallflower, larkspur, sweet william and French marigold. The second, cheaper, collection (at 1s 6d) included only six varieties, whilst the very cheapest (at only 1s) contained the essentials of nigella, sweet pea, mignonette and pink malope. In each case, the nigella was the variety Miss Jekyll, named after the garden designer and plantswoman Gertrude Jekyll.

As well as being present by name in the most popular of children's garden flowers, Gertrude Jekyll also encouraged children to garden for themselves. Her own love of flowers and gardens had been nurtured as a young girl when, armed with a copy of *Flowers of the Field* by the Reverend C.A. Johns, she had roamed through the wild meadows and hedgerows identifying plants. The Reverend Johns had also written a book specifically on gardening for children (in 1849), although it was not this that attracted the young Jekyll, but the far more difficult botanical work. In later life, Jekyll called it one of the three books that had given her the most pleasure in her life. Her own book for children, *Children and Gardens* (1908), is one of the very few written from a child's perspective, despite being published when Jekyll was, in her own words, "quite an old woman" (in fact she was 64). Memories of her own childhood fill the pages, evoking a Victorian garden with its shrubberies and lawns. Perhaps thinking back to the royal gardens at Osborne House, Jekyll recommends not only a separate garden but a small playhouse (with parlour, kitchen and pantry) to go with it, in which the children can "keep house and cook and receive their friends" although, as she admits, it is a somewhat costly toy. An earlier version of this luxury children's playhouse and garden had been created by Earl de Grey at his mansion at Wrest Park, Bedfordshire in 1856 and can still be seen there. Less costly was Jekyll's suggestion that a child's first foray into gardening should be in the form of growing their own name in mustard and cress.

BELOW: Nigella Miss Jekyll was often recommended as a suitable flower for children's gardens.

BOTTOM: A 1930s' children's toy garden that could be used on its own or as part of a dolls' house.

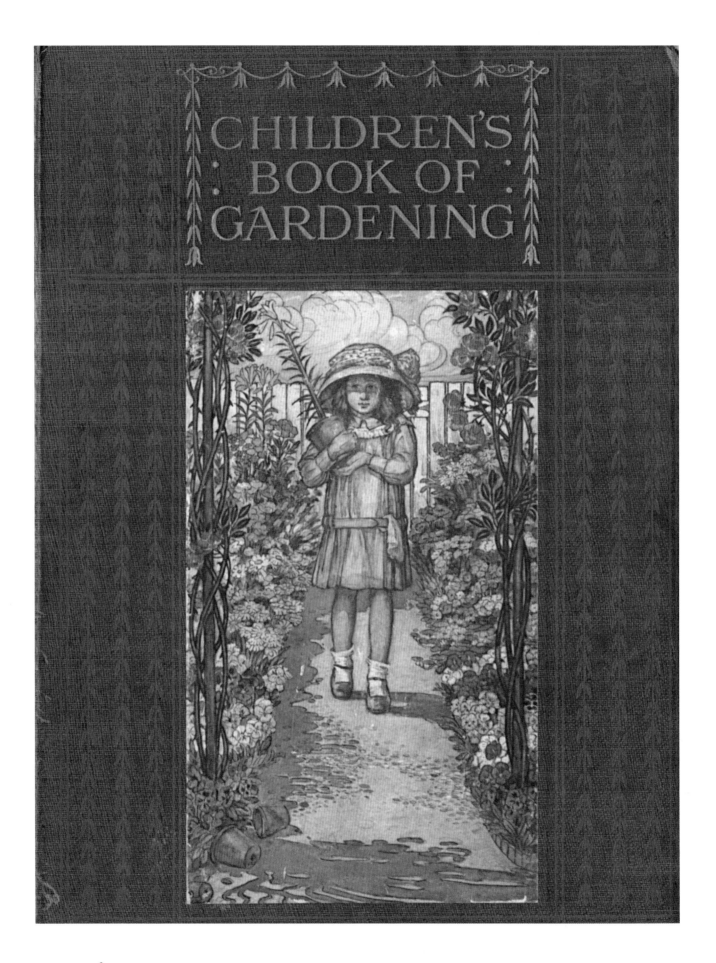

As well as seeds, other marketing opportunities associated with the fashion for children's gardens included the small tools made by companies such as Britans. By the 1930s, manufactured tools had come to replace the hand-made tools of the nineteenth century. Children's tools included everything from watering cans to lawnmowers (although even these were not as dangerous as Gertrude Jekyll's suggestion that children whittled their own wooden tool handles!) and gardens for dolls' houses, replete with miniature flowers and flower beds to stick them in.

The publication of Frances Hodgson Burnett's *The Secret Garden* in 1911 introduced thousands more children to the delights of a garden. Still a much-loved and often reprinted book, the story tells of the orphaned Mary, her mysteriously ill cousin Colin and the mystical half-wild boy Dickon. The book is centred around the neglected walled garden of the title, where Mary discovers love and a new life as the garden awakens over the long spring and summer months. A deeply religious tale of loss and resurrection, it appealed to both children and parents of the period. Descriptions of Dickon's purchase of the flower seeds (mignonette, white poppies and larkspur) for a penny a packet, the discovery of the buds and the final flowering of the roses became part of childhood, a romantic vision apart from the practicalities of the radishes and carrots on the school plot.

School gardens were to be given an unexpected morale boost with the outbreak of the First World War in 1914. Although the need to "grow your own" was not recognized immediately, the U-boat blockades of 1917 saw school gardens everywhere helping out with the war effort. The most famous of these was perhaps at Eton, where the school playing fields were dug up. The vegetables from these school allotment gardens supplied the school kitchens, and the boys themselves worked up hearty appetites digging them. For many, this would have been their first – and perhaps their only – encounter with hard manual labour, unless of course their Edwardian parents had seen fit to create children's gardens at home. All around the country, existing school gardens were expanded and in some schools the girls as well as the boys were asked to join in the gardening lessons for the first time, echoing the efforts of the Women's Land Army on farms and market gardens.

The growth of the suburbs and garden cities in the late Edwardian and inter-war period saw gardens become a cherished status symbol for many middle-class families. The ideal nuclear family gardened together, with father and sons doing the digging and pruning, while mother and daughters weeded and snipped at flower-heads. Gardening tools for children were easily available

ABOVE: The popular image of "girl with watering can" appeared in many guises – paintings, books and advertisements etc. This cut-out was a scrap produced for a Victorian scrapbook c. 1880.

OPPOSITE: *The Children's Book of Gardening* was a joint undertaking by three women: Mrs Sidgwick and Mrs Paynter wrote the text whilst Mrs Cayley-Robinson provided illustrations.

and relatively cheap by the late Edwardian period. The tools that Dickon bought in *The Secret Garden* were said to cost only 2s for a child's spade, rake, fork and trowel set. However, as fashions changed in gardens generally, and annual bedding gave way to herbaceous borders, gardening became less child-friendly and less instant in its rewards; although the mustard and cress initials could still be sown by the youngest along with a sprinkling of love-in-the-mist. Enid Blyton, the famous children's author, released a book called *The Children's Garden* in 1935 (re-issued after the war as *Let's Garden*). Schools continued to teach nature studies through the 1930s, although only the rural areas considered it as a providing a probable career for their younger pupils, and increasingly gardening was tied to science rather than to nature and productivity. All that was to change on the outbreak of the Second World War in 1939 and the launch of the Dig for Victory campaign.

The outbreak of the Second World War galvanized Britain into gardening action, including the children. All over the country, lawns were dug up for vegetable plots and allotments were laid out on school playing fields and public parks. As conscription started to bite, a campaign was launched to get children

SOWING THE SEED: GARDENING FOR CHILDREN

to do their bit to feed the nation. Soon cinema-goers were treated to Pathé newsreels of children digging up bomb-sites in the East End of London to create allotments: wielding pickaxes and forks in a way calculated to result in injury rather than crops. Featured in the government's media campaign was Jimmy West, an 11-year-old who had supposedly come back from evacuation to help with the war effort. Jimmy and his chums were sowing seeds sent to them from America, turning the ruins of the Blitz into gardens for all. Bethnal Green Bombed Sites Association arranged the land permits for the scheme and provided the tools, and the Webbe Boys Club did the training. In the hidden bombed-out basements, Pathé news recorded whole armies of children who tended flowers and vegetables and even kept rabbits and hens. Most children either helped out on the allotment or in the garden – although the traditional flower-filled children's garden was abandoned or put to better use to grow lettuce and salad. Having a large school garden where children could be sent to work off their energies was essential in the over-crowded rural schools that received evacuees. Some schools almost doubled the numbers of pupils and the school garden was a vital means of providing food for all the extra mouths.

BELOW: Even urban schools had their vegetable gardens, as recorded here in the early twentieth century with its tall fence. The bean poles at the far end disappear into the trees.

At Oving (West Sussex), the parochial school laid out 12 plots in the vicarage garden across the road, with a boy and a girl in charge of each, whilst pupils at the Merchant Taylor's School at Ashwell (Hertfordshire) had to dig up all the flower beds and replace them with vegetable plots, as well as cultivating an extra three acres outside the school grounds.

Many schools made the vegetable plots competitive, with a different class in charge of each one. Moulsecombe School in Brighton had school allotments close to the mortuary chapel and each class vied to outdo the others in crops. Most of the children came from rural backgrounds in the Sussex countryside and knew more about crops and farming than their teachers. However, for urban children from the London East End, evacuation might give them their first experience of gardening or of the idea that vegetables actually came from the ground.

The school garden outlasted the end of the war and carried on into the

ABOVE: With the aid of a Sutton's special seed collection for children, a garden border could overflow with colour in the summer.

RIGHT: By the late 1930s nature had started to give way to science in the school garden as this collection of school radio broadcasts by Cecil Middleton indicates.

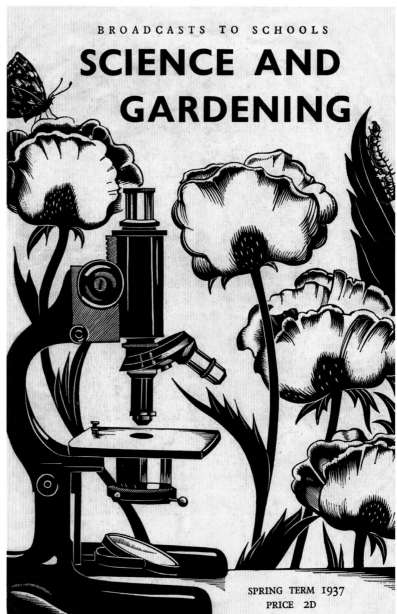

BROADCASTS TO SCHOOLS

SCIENCE AND GARDENING

SPRING TERM 1937
PRICE 2D

austerity years that followed it, but by the 1960s the delightful hours spent sowing radishes in the sunshine were denied to many, as new school buildings, built to cope with the baby-boomers, were constructed over the traditional plots. Although primary and junior schools maintained the tradition of hands-on growing, especially in rural areas, learning became more classroom focused. Children's gardens, both at home and in school, were a neglected fashion, spurned in favour of television (and then computers) until the revival of interest in the first decade of the twenty-first century.

ABOVE This colourful poster of a school vegetable garden in the 1950s would soon be regarded as old fashioned and anachronistic as playing fields and gardens were replaced with tarmac and buildings.

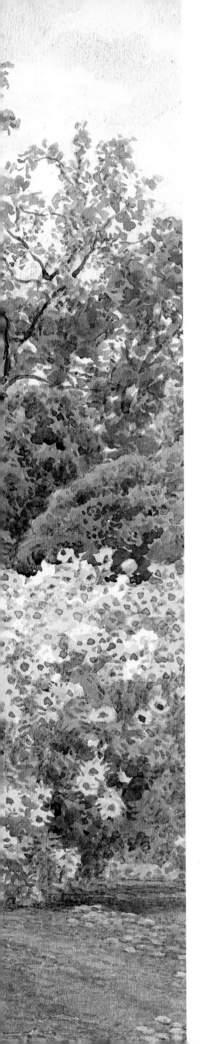

4

The Garden Beautiful: Edwardian Extravagance

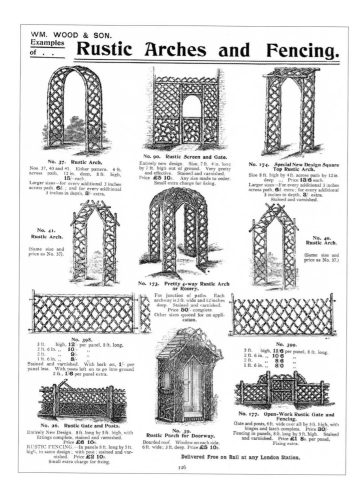

WM. WOOD & SON.
Examples
of . .

Rustic Arches and Fencing.

No. 37. Rustic Arch.
Nos. 37, 40 and 41. Either pattern. 4 ft. across path, 12 in. deep, 8 ft. high, **15**/- each.
Larger sizes—for every additional 3 inches across path, **6**d.; and for every additional 3 inches in depth, **3**/- extra.

No. 90. Rustic Screen and Gate.
Entirely new design. Size, 7 ft. 4 in. long by 7 ft. high out of ground. Very pretty and effective. Stained and varnished. Price **£5 10**s. Any size made to order. Small extra charge for fixing.

No. 174. Special New Design Square Top Rustic Arch.
Size 8 ft. high by 4 ft. across path by 12 in. deep ... Price **13/6** each.
Larger sizes—For every additional 3 inches across path, **6**d.; for every additional 3 inches in depth, **3**/- extra. Stained and varnished.

No. 41. Rustic Arch.
(Same size and price as No. 37).

No. 173. Pretty 4-way Rustic Arch or Rosery.
For junction of paths. Each archway is 5 ft. wide and 12 inches deep. Stained and varnished. Price **50**/- complete. Other sizes quoted for on application.

No. 40. Rustic Arch.
(Same size and price as No. 37.)

No. 398.
3 ft. high, **12**/- per panel, 8 ft. long.
2 ft. 6 in. ,, **10**/- ,,
2 ft. ,, **9**/- ,,
1 ft. 6 in. ,, **8**/- ,,
Stained and varnished. With bark on, **1**/- per panel less. With posts left on to go into ground 2 ft., **1/6** per panel extra.

No. 39. Rustic Porch for Doorway.
Boarded roof. Window on each side. 6 ft. wide; 3 ft. deep. Price **£5 10**s.

No. 399.
3 ft. high, **11/6** per panel, 8 ft. long.
2 ft. 6 in. ,, **10/6** ,,
2 ft. ,, **8/6** ,,
1 ft. 6 in. ,, **8/0** ,,

No. 26. Rustic Gate and Posts.
Entirely New Design. 8 ft. long by 5 ft. high, with fittings complete, stained and varnished. Price **£6 10**s.
RUSTIC FENCING.—In panels 8 ft. long by 5 ft. high, in same design ; with post ; stained and varnished. Price **£2 10**s. Small extra charge for fixing.

No. 177. Open-Work Rustic Gate and Fencing.
Gate and posts, 4 ft. wide over all by 3 ft. high, with hinges and latch complete. Price **30**/-
Fencing in panels, 8 ft. long by 3 ft. high. Stained and varnished. Price **£1 8**s. per panel. Fixing extra.

Delivered Free on Rail at any London Station.

126

PREVIOUS PAGE: This idyllic image of a cottage at Ockham (Surrey) is by the artist Thomas Hunn and dates to 1909. Hunn also painted parts of Gertrude Jekyll's garden at Munstead Wood.

ABOVE: The fashion for rustic continued from the Victorian period through the Edwardian, fitting in rather better with the "natural" design of this period than the formal beds of the Victorian garden.

RIGHT: Perhaps awaiting his love by the rustic bower?

In contrast to the Victorian love of bright colours and order in the garden, the Edwardian garden was a place of art and craft, fruitfulness and rural fantasy. Roses tumbled over rustic trellises, water lilies luxuriated in sunken ponds, and peaches pollinated under the artful care of a gardener armed with a rabbit's foot. Although the backlash against bedding had started as early as the 1870s, it was the Edwardians who ushered in the "Garden Beautiful", leading nature by the hand. In the words of Walter Wright, author of *Beautiful Gardens* (1907) and the surprisingly poetic Horticultural Superintendent of the Kent County Council, a garden may "open the gates of a new and beautiful world, a world in which imagination and illusion play an allied part with all the vigour and abandon of youth".

In keeping with the tenets of the Arts and Crafts movement – which championed the use of traditional methods and materials and the association of landscape and house – Walter Wright argued that the the garden and house should combine together, the one growing from the other, both composed of the local landscape in the popular vernacular style. "Our Ideal Garden shall come close to the walls of the house, and linger lovingly there, as though it were indeed a part and parcel of our home. It shall caress the walls, lay tender fingers upon the windows, and spray itself across the threshold," he wrote. Even the air was to be infused with the garden, as "Our Ideal Garden shall be a garden of perfume ... that recalls more swiftly and vividly a happy incident or scene of childhood or youth." Pergolas, serpentine walks and bulb-planted orchards were the styles of the day, and gardens described as "old-fashioned" were the height of Edwardian fashion. Roses and peonies became favourite plants, with lavenders and jasmines adding even more scent and colour. Grey foliage flattered the mellow

pathways of the Arts and Crafts home, creating an illusion of warmth, and the tradition of the herb garden flourished with its *Helichrysum* (curry plant) and *Stachys lanata* (also known as lamb's ears or rabbit's ears).

> *Not the smallest and dryest garden should be without* Stachys lanata, *a white wooly leaved plant, called rabbit's ears by cottage children, and particularly attractive to some people, who through life retain the love of a child for something wooly and soft … These leaves were formerly used as edging to beds in a very objectionable way; but when grown in large clumps they are most useful for picking.*

> *Theresa Earle,* Pot Pourri from a Surrey Garden *(1897)*

William Robinson (1838–1935) was vehement in his hatred of brightly coloured annual bedding and equally passionate in his love of hardy plants and the "wild garden". Although his most famous books came out in the Victorian period, the "father of the English flower garden" was at his most influential through periodicals such as *Cottage Gardening* and *Gardening Illustrated*, which he wrote and edited into the Edwardian period from his old manor house at Gravetye, Sussex. Gravetye was famous for the clematis clambering over the walls, the woodland gardens underplanted with spring bulbs, and the tufted pansies beloved of its owner. Gertrude Jekyll was one of many who were influenced by Robinson, ensuring that his love of hardy plants became the backbone of so many Edwardian gardens, from cottages to manor houses. Although Robinson himself denied it, the style of his own garden also fitted well with the passion for all things Italianate in the first decade of the twentieth

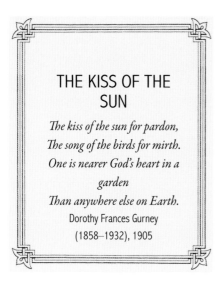

RIGHT: Lawrence Johnston gardened at both Hidcote and Serre de la Madone (France) using plants appropriate to the climate at each site. Norah Lindsay was a close friend and frequent visitor to Hidcote, along with her daughter Nancy.

century, with its combination of weathered stone and overflowing shrubs. His was not an architectural garden of topiary and marble columns, and yet the pergola and the terrace with its stone steps and square summerhouse hinted at warmer climes.

The idea of the Renaissance villa captivated the Edwardian upper classes, so many of whom travelled to villas on the Italian Riviera or to Florence for the season. Once home, they created the English dream of the Italian villa garden. In the words of Edith Wharton, the author of *Italian Villas and their Gardens* (1904), that dream was a combination of "marble, water and perennial verdure". Amongst those that followed the dream, at least in part, were Lawrence Johnston (1871–1958) in his famous gardens at Hidcote (Gloucestershire) and Harold Peto (1854–1933) at Iford Manor (Wiltshire). Whilst Johnston was a plant collector, travelling to China and South America, Peto was a collector of objects, and the terrace behind his house was full of urns and pillars, interspersed with cypresses and rosemary. At Cliveden (Buckinghamshire), William Waldorf Astor and his politician wife, Nancy, even brought the original balustrade from the Villa Borghese back from Rome to grace their garden terrace. The novelist Robert Louis Stevenson captured the ideal

garden in words when he wrote: "The old flowers are the best and should grow carelessly in corners. Indeed the ideal fortune is to find an old garden, once very richly cared for, since sunk into neglect, and to tend, not repair, that neglect."

For those intent on the sentiment of the garden, rather than its architectural inheritance, there was always the cottage garden style, one which could be neatly combined with Arts and Crafts for those with sufficient money to buy trellises and arches, or left with only humble brick or tile edging for those without the means. Both Jekyll and Robinson felt there was much to learn from a cottage garden. Jekyll declared that: "Not infrequently in passing along a country road, with eye alert to note the beauties that are so often presented by little wayside cottage gardens, something is seen that may well serve as a lesson in better planting. The lesson is generally one that teaches simplicity." Cottage garden style was promoted through the popular watercolours of artists such as Helen Allingham (1848–1926), Thomas Hunn (1857–1928) and Myles Birkett Foster (1825–99). Foster's depictions of cottage life and gardening illustrated the popular book *In Rustic England* which came out in 1906, while Helen Allingham embellished the even more sentimental *Happy England* (1903).

Watercolours depicted an idyllic rural life where ducklings and kittens fought their way through forests of cabbages and sweet williams, and women paused in their work with baskets full of immaculately white washing. Although sentimental in taste, the paintings were often drawn from life – perhaps with the later addition of the ducklings and kittens – and the depictions of flowers are clear enough for identification of the most popular cottage plants. The watercolourist Beatrice Parsons was so accurate that she was hired by seed companies to illustrate their packets and catalogues, and was asked by Ernest Cook to illustrate his book *Gardens of England* in 1908, yet another volume that fed the Edwardian gardener's dream of overflowing flower borders, sundials and old-fashioned dovecotes.

Towering over the Edwardian garden, at least in design terms if not in stature,

RIGHT: As her eyesight deteriorated, Gertrude Jekyll often gave advice by letter rather than visiting a client's home. Here she instructs on "wall gardening".

FAR RIGHT: The artist Helen Allingham was a friend of Gertrude Jekyll's and recorded her magnificent 200-foot- (60-metre-) long flower borders.

BELOW: Gertrude Jekyll's potting-shed desk, which is now housed in the Garden Museum.

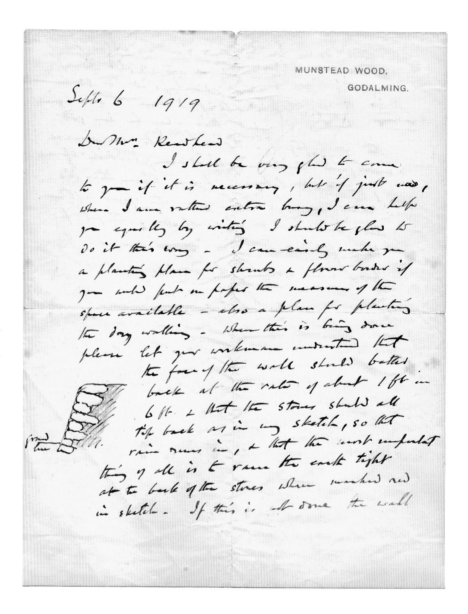

was the artist, plantswoman and author Gertrude Jekyll. From her own Surrey garden at Munstead Wood, she influenced the nation's gardens through her writings and designs. Born in London in 1843, Jeykll's first love was art and she attended the South Kensington School of Art, creating watercolours and, later, inlay work and embroidery in the Arts and Crafts style. Her studies brought her into contact with artists such as John Ruskin, William Morris and Lord Leighton; the latter even bought her embroideries for his magnificently decorated house and studio. Jekyll's parents promoted her artistic talent and encouraged her to travel on the Continent, where she enriched her understanding of the effect of light and shade on colour tones. On the death of her father in 1876, the family returned to Surrey, and by the late 1880s gardening and garden-writing had overtaken art in her life, or rather had combined with art, as her garden design was one where the artist's palette ruled. Colour schemes were fundamental to her designs, carefully orchestrated and using knowledge gained from study of the

THE GARDEN BEAUTIFUL: EDWARDIAN EXTRAVAGANCE

RIGHT: As well as herbaceous borders, Jekyll's garden at Munstead Wood contained separate garden areas for grouping of seasonal plants or particular colour themes. Here the lupin and iris garden is in full bloom.

colour-wheel of contrasts and complements: purples highlighting yellows; cool blues stretching out distances; and hot architectural reds. Her plantsmanship brought her into contact with men such as William Robinson, the rosarian Dean Reynolds Hole and the rhododendron specialist Harry Mangles. It was at a tea party with Harry Mangles that she met the young architect Edwin Lutyens, whom she influenced with her love of vernacular architecture and the "Surrey style" and with whom she was to work in partnership from 1893 until the outbreak of the First World War.

Although Jekyll was essentially Victorian by birth, and her first gardening articles were written in the 1870s, her major influence was not felt until the Edwardian period. As late as 1897, Theresa Earle, herself a Surrey gardener, commented that she hoped some of Miss Jekyll's articles in the *Guardian* "will be republished in book form" so that other gardeners might become aware of them. In Mrs Earle's eyes, Jekyll was a relative newcomer and she records that Jekyll "has gone through the stage so common to all ambitious and enthusiastic amateurs, of trying to grow everything, and of often wasting much precious room in growing inferior plants, or plants which, even though they may be worth growing in themselves, are yet not worth the care and feeding which a light soil necessitates if they are to be successful."

Heartening though it is to hear of the early mistakes of horticultural heroines, by the Edwardian period Jekyll was one of the most influential of designers and hardy plant borders were the essential element in any garden. For those with large enough gardens, her signature border was an exercise in colour

GARDENING AS FINE ART

"I am strongly of the opinion that the possession of a quantity of plants, however good the plants may be themselves, and however ample their number, does not make a garden; it only makes a collection ... and it seems to me that the duty we owe to our gardens and to our own bettering in our gardens is so to use the plants that they shall form beautiful pictures ... It is just in the way it is done that lies the whole difference between commonplace gardening and gardening that may rightly claim to rank as fine art."

Gertrude Jekyll, Colour Schemes for the Flower Garden *(1921)*

JUNE BOR

THE GARDEN BEAUTIFUL: EDWARDIAN EXTRAVAGANCE

S OF LUPIN AND IRIS IN THE GARDEN AT MUNSTEAD WOOD.

toning, with whites and greys progressing through pale pinks and yellows, then to the oranges and burgundy, and finally a central blaze of crimson and scarlet before gradually subsiding again. At her own garden at Munstead Wood, the scheme took up a border 200 feet (60 metres) long by 14 feet (4 metres) wide, but those with more modest suburban homes could always adapt.

Single-colour gardens were also one of her hallmarks, and Jekyll's grey foliage garden was visited by Vita Sackville-West long before the Sissinghurst white garden made its appearance.

Although a Jekyll-and-Lutyens-designed garden was the preserve of the few (although perhaps not that few – as she designed almost 400 gardens!), many more were influenced through her prolific writings, which, as Theresa Earle had predicted, were soon brought together in a series of books published through the Edwardian period, including *Lilies for English Gardens* (1901), *Roses for English Gardens* (1902), *Colour in the Flower Garden* (1908), *Children and Gardens* (1908) and *Gardens for Small Country Houses* (1912).

Not everyone was enamoured of the Jekyll style of long herbaceous or flower borders. In his *Memoirs of an Aesthete,* Harold Acton recalled visiting the

2270 Kew Gardens. The American Gardens.

ABOVE: Topisary was another popular feature of Edwardian gardens. Here an apt teapot advertises Mrs West's Tea Gardens.

BELOW: A typical long border design in Gertrude Jekyll's own hand. Note her use of drifts of plants. This design is for Appletree Farm.

gardens of Lady Battersea in 1914. He records that: "The flowers were superb, the lawns like carpets, yet I was disappointed. Evidently flowers alone make a garden in England. This was my first sight of herbaceous borders, a riot of colour which I failed to appreciate; they seemed to be stacked higgledy-piggledy, like counters at a country fair. One wandered beside them, attracted by a lupin here, a lobelia there, feeling more of a bee than a human thing." One can only hope that Acton was never invited to a garden party at Munstead Wood!

Although herbaceous borders and perennial plantings ruled the roost for many Edwardian gardeners, other fashions crept in during the first decade of the twentieth century. Among these, the vogue for Japanese gardens was perhaps the most influential, although American planting was also popular

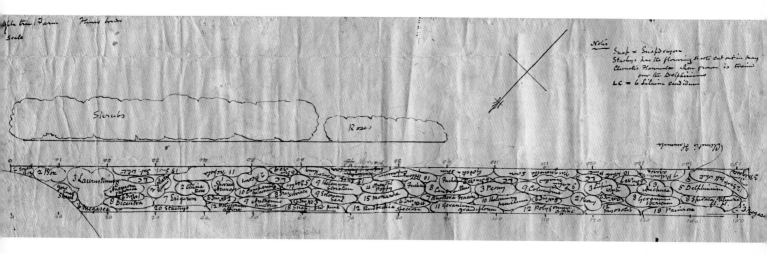

Garden of the Floating Isle

In the Japanese Gardens,
Japan-British Exhibition, London, 1910.

THE GARDEN BEAUTIFUL: EDWARDIAN EXTRAVAGANCE

OPPOSITE ABOVE: The 1910 Japanese–British Exhibition included gardens created by Japanese designers and a backdrop of Mount Fuji on a painted cloth.

OPPOSITE BELOW LEFT: Japanese anemone (*Anemone hupehensis* var. *japonica*) was discovered in China by the planthunter Robert Fortune in 1844.

OPPOSITE BELOW RIGHT: This wonderful wicker barrow reflects the fascination with Arts and Crafts but would have been more ornamental than practical.

RIGHT: The essential elements of an English Japanese garden according to Richard Sudell in *The New Illustrated Gardening Encyclopaedia*.

JAPANESE GARDENS

among the upper classes who could afford to convert their gardens to the acidic soils that many of the trees and shrubs associated with that style (if not actually with America) necessitated.

Japanese-style gardens – usually no more than an embellishment with a Japanese flowering cherry, a wisteria or an artfully placed stone lantern – had first become popular in the late nineteenth century as the opening up of Japanese trade slowly let ideas from that country infiltrate all parts of European culture. Gilbert and Sullivan's comic opera *The Mikado*, first performed in 1885, was part of the same fashion. Native Japanese plants were still quite rare and expensive but some bamboos and a pool with water lilies could be accomplished even by those with quite modest incomes. In reality, many of the plants, such as the Japanese anemone (*Anemone hupehensis* var. *japonica*), were actually from China. Others had already been familiars in the English garden for decades if not centuries, following the earlier fashion for chinoiserie in the eighteenth century. In fact, any plant whose Latin name ended in *japonica, sinensis* or *orientalis* might be thrown into the mix. By 1901, the nurserymen V. N. Gauntlett & Co offered stone lanterns of various sizes and styles and a range of bronze cranes to stand by the edge of the pool, all direct from Japan. By 1906, Gauntlett & Co had become the Japanese nurserymen, supplying both Japanese plants and the complete set of authentic props.

In 1910 the opening of the Japanese–British Exhibition at White City in West London took place. It included a series of "authentic" Japanese gardens below a huge painted backdrop of snow-capped mountains, inspiring wealthy visitors to further efforts. Trend-setting shops such as Liberty's of London joined the craze, selling stone lanterns, thatched bamboo teahouses, Japanese lacquered garden furniture, Japanese-style bridges and the inevitable bronze cranes. Notable Japanese-style private gardens of the period included that at Tatton Park (Cheshire), almost certainly inspired by Alan de Tatton's visit to the 1910 exhibition; at Friar Park (Oxfordshire), a Japanese garden joined the collection of rock gardens, medieval gardens and topiary gardens all created by the eccentric Sir Frank Crisp, whilst Gatton Park, Surrey, owned by the mustard magnate Jeremiah Colman, boasted pools, lanterns, stepping stones, cascades and a teahouse, although at least one of the lanterns was installed the wrong way up, having been put together from Japanese components by the very English head gardener. Hinchingbrooke House (Huntingdonshire) not only had "Japanese planting", a pond and a bronze crane, but the added attraction of an erupting Mount Fuji which could be detonated by a discretely hidden servant whilst visitors were being shown the garden.

Even before their eventual fall from popularity in the aftermath of the Japanese attack on Pearl Harbor in the Second World War, Japanese gardens had their detractors. In 1917, Lawrence Weaver wrote in the newly popular *Country Life* (founded in 1897):

> *The importation of exotic motifs into garden design in England is dangerous; not only because they are rarely understood, but because there are few sites where they can take their place at all naturally. The disposition of a few typical ornaments, of a bronze stork here and a stone lantern there, does not make a Japanese garden; it only makes an English garden speak with a Japanese accent.*

Others couched their criticisms in more judicious terms. On being shown round one of the more ambitious of the Japanese-style gardens in England at Gunnersbury, west London, the then ambassador for Japan was apparently heard to say, "We have nothing like it in Japan."

The rather inauspicious year of 1913 saw the first ever flowering of the Chelsea Flower Show, now beloved of millions and known around the world. The Royal Horticultural Society (RHS) had first been founded as far back as 1804, originally as The Horticultural Society of London, by the renowned naturalist and botanist Sir Joseph Banks and the scientist John Wedgwood of the famous Wedgwood pottery family. The first floral fêtes, as they were then known, were held at the Duke of Devonshire's estate in Chiswick rather than at Chelsea. The Duke was also an enthusiastic horticulturalist alongside his head gardener, Joseph Paxton. In 1861, Prince Albert granted the society a royal charter and the RHS was born, complete with a new garden headquarters at Kensington. The Edwardian period saw further changes and increasing popular recognition of the society. In 1903, the society was gifted its now famous garden at Wisley for experimental planting and breeding. The following year, 1904, saw the society's centenary and opening of offices at Vincent Square, London, which also housed the Lindley Library based on the collection of John Lindley (originally acquired in 1866).

Since its move to Kensington in 1862, the society had used its gardens there for its Great Spring Show, but in 1888 it chose instead the more central site of the Temple Gardens. This was a huge success, with five marquees exhibiting the best of Victorian (and then Edwardian) gardening. In 1912, however, the show was replaced by the Royal International Horticultural Exhibition, which was so large that it could not be accommodated in the Temple grounds. Instead, those of the Royal Hospital Chelsea were

ABOVE: Carters' Seeds created a rhododendron walk for their Chelsea exhibition in 1914. The show continued into the first years of the war but was absent in 1917 and 1918.

LEFT: Whilst the spring show was held at Chelsea, the great RHS Summer Show was held at Holland House during the first decades of the twentieth century.

RIGHT: In 1912 the annual RHS show was replaced by the Royal Horticultural International Show — and gnomes crept in for the first (and last) time in the famous "Chelsea" marquees.

ABOVE: The garden beautiful could also be the garden bountiful as cheap labour filled the kitchen gardens.

requisitioned by the great nurseryman Sir Harry Veitch. The extra space that Chelsea gave was a huge hit.

Despite the outbreak of the First World War, the Chelsea Show continued in 1914, 1915 and 1916 but was cancelled in 1917 and 1918 as conditions worsened. The post-war period saw it back in full bloom and, with royal visits and Chelsea tea parties becoming a tradition, it was set to last at least until the next war. The Second World War had a greater impact as blockades hit hard and nurseries and seedsmen were forced to grow vegetables instead of flowers. Resumption of the show was delayed until 1947, but its eventual return was heralded as a great success.

Edward VII died in 1910, but the "garden beautiful" lived on until the outbreak of war in August 1914. The first impact on gardens was the loss

BELOW: Although the RHS shows dominated the seasons, most towns had their own "great shows", as recorded in this advertisement for Fertilo. Pansies, shown here with sweet williams and asters, were the favourite of Edwardian plantsman William Robinson.

BOTTOM: Victorian innovation and Edwardian pride combined to produce an array of fruit and vegetables.

of staff as men volunteered to join up, often following their employers or their sons into the local regiments. Many lost their lives in the trenches during the first two years of the war, and March 1916 saw the introduction of conscription for men aged between 18 and 41 (eventually extended to 51). Men who had spent their whole lives tending orchids and nurturing pineapples found themselves transported to the muddy battlefields of the Western Front. Throughout the land, the kitchen gardens and pleasure grounds, so dependent on their large labour force, fell silent. Garden owners who had previously reckoned on employing a man and a "garden boy'" for every acre of productive ground were now reduced to an elderly working head gardener with as many village boys as they could get. In August 1915, the gardening staff at Heligan (Cornwall) signed their names on the wall of the gardeners' "thunder box" before setting off for the front line. Of the 22 gardeners employed before the war, 16 were to die on the fields of Flanders, leaving behind them the magnificent gardens with their melon pits and rhododendrons, and the half-completed Japanese garden. On the grand estate of Luton Hoo (Bedfordshire), 99 members of staff were called up, of whom 22 were from the gardens; 16 staff members were killed, including three gardeners.

Whilst the trenches swallowed so many of the skilled gardeners, the need on the Home Front became pressing. In 1917, Kaiser Wilhelm II issued orders to German U-boat commanders to "frighten the British flag off the face of the waters and starve the British people until they ... will kneel and

THE GARDEN BEAUTIFUL: EDWARDIAN EXTRAVAGANCE

POTATOES CARRO... CABBAGE ONIONS

I hav'nt got a gardening Plot
But Still as you can see
I'm managing to grow enough
To suit just You and Me.

1915

Hobbies

GOLD MEDAL ROSES, SEEDS &

HOBBIES LIMITED
NORFOLK NURSERIES
DEREHAM
ALSO 17, BROAD ST. PLACE. LONDON. E.C.

BY ROYAL APPOINTMENT

plead". Not expecting a blockade, the British government had not prepared for a food war, and hasty arrangements were made to produce food on the Home Front. As it would be during the Second World War, the government's focus included small-scale family production and allotments in particular, which became a prominent part of the food campaign; more than two million of them were cultivated by the end of the war. For the first time ever, growing your own vegetables became a fashion amongst the middle classes as well as a necessity for labouring families.

ABOVE LEFT: Gardening staff such as these would soon be lining up for very different duties as men between 18 and 41 were conscripted to the trenches.

ABOVE RIGHT: Hobbies Nurseries of Dereham produced this very patriotic catalogue In the first spring of the war.

5

Ladies in Bloomers: Women and the Garden

90 YEARS' PROGRESS

BUTCHER'S

SEED AND BULB

CATALOGUE

Season
1954

From the medieval period to the nineteenth century, the humble housewife was often in charge of the day-to-day matters of the kitchen garden. Raising food for the pot and herbs for the medicine cupboard, hers was a largely thankless task. In the words of the sixteenth-century garden writer Thomas Tusser, "Good housewives provide, ere a sickness do come, of sundrie good things in her house to have some; ... Cold Herbs in her garden for agues that burn, that over strong heat to good temper may turn." In order to ensure her garden was full of the herbs and vegetables, the housewife might also take note of Tusser's admonition that:

> *In March and in April, from morning to night,*
> *in sowing and setting, good housewives delight:*
> *To have in a garden, or other like plot,*
> *to turn up their houses, or to furnish their pot.*
> *The nature of flowers Dame Physic doth show,*
> *she teacheth them all to be known to a few.*
> *To set or to sow, or else sown to remove,*
> *how that should be practised, learn if you love.*

Instructions for digging, weeding, sowing, weeding, watering and gathering (by the waxing and waning of the moon) followed, with reference to dibber, line, rake, mattock and spade (forks were not yet in use).

Maids might also be expected to carry out weeding duties for their mistress, although the garden writer William Lawson advised in his *Country Housewives' Garden* (1618) that "the mistress [should] either be present herself, or teach her maids to know herbs from weeds". The "good housewives" that made up Lawson's readership might include within their ranks some who actually gardened for a living. Weeding in particular is one way in which women have been able to earn an honest wage down the ages. Using quick nimble fingers, often adorned with steel-tipped finger gloves, women might earn 3d a day in the sixteenth century, a wage that in some places does not appear to have risen until the mid-eighteenth century! The royal gardens at Hampton Court had a team of women weeders in the Tudor period, kept busy removing dandelions, docks, thistle, dodder, nettles and groundsel – all carefully recorded in the royal records. Weeding remained a possible "career" for women well into the nineteenth century, but the advent of the bothy system whereby the gardeners for large country houses all lived in, meant that women were no longer employed except as occasional casual labour or in smaller establishments.

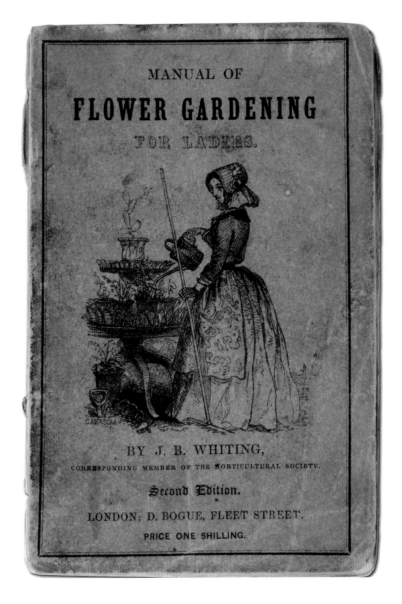

Amongst the more refined classes, where women were ladies and weeds were delegated to the maids, an interest in rare plants and flowers was encouraged from as early as the eighteenth century. Flower painting, botanical studies and plant-collecting (in particular ferns and other less showy plants) were encouraged as polite accomplishments. Some ladies even went as far as embellishing grottoes and ornamenting summerhouses, although most concentrated on the nurturing of the flower garden or conservatory. One of the most famous of these ladies of accomplishment was Mary Delany (1700–88). From a family that had fallen from favour on the death of Queen Anne, Mary's life was a turbulent one. A forced marriage to a much older man ensued, but after his death, Mary remained a widow until her flight to Ireland in 1743 with the suitor of her choice from a lower class. She was finally reintegrated into the court life where her hobbies of grotto creation and flower embroidery

ABOVE: A jardinière stand such as this allowed women to indulge a passion for flower gardens while remaining fashionably dressed and respectably indoors!

ABOVE: Although placed outdoors, tending this stand did not involve the wearer in any bending — which is just as well given the size of the hat and the tightness of her waist.

RIGHT: Only the most careful of gardeners can wear white, and yet it was an essential dress colour for unmarried Victorian females, yet another impediment to active gardening.

created a fashion. Her most famous works were her paper collages of flowers, which were so lifelike that the naturalist Sir Joseph Banks ensured she was kept supplied with newly introduced rarities to record for posterity in her own unique way. In his celebrated epic *The Botanic Garden* (written in 1789–91), the famous Erasmus Darwin dedicated a verse of a poem entitled "The Loves of the Flowers" to a description of Mrs Delany at work, surrounded by her "virgin train" of protégées:

So now DELANY forms her mimic bowers,
Her paper foliage, and her silken flowers;
Her virgin train the tender scissors ply,
Vein the green leaf, the purple petal dye.

Mary Delany was not alone in her love of plants; Lady Luxborough at Barrells Hall, Eleanor Butler and Sarah Ponsonby ("The Ladies of Llangollen") at Plas Newydd, Marchioness Grey at Wrest Park, and Margaret, Duchess of Portland, at Bulstrode, were all avid gardeners or plant collectors in their own way. These aristocratic ladies set a fashion that was to touch the lives of their Victorian "sisters", liberating them from the lifelessness of their suburban sitting rooms.

By the Victorian period, a whole new category of suburban lady gardeners had come into being, neither the wholesome country housewife with her herb-lore nor the aristocratic flower lover, but instead women anxious to improve their lives by a little healthy exercise. For many a middle-class suburban wife or spinster, life could be stultifyingly boring. Trapped in a social class where status was measured by the number of servants and the tightness of your corset, there was often little to do and less reason to do it yourself. Whilst cottage housewives still harvested their little plot, for the middle-class woman, vegetables were something the cook dealt with. The movement to gardening started only slowly, building on the acceptable accomplishments of botany and flower studies.

A fashion for conservatories and "winter gardens" to house botanical specimens meant that women could garden without being seen outside or needing anything more outrageous than an apron and a small potting trowel. Any alarm at the overtly sexual nature of plants such as orchids and lilies was countered by the craze for ferns (*pteridomania*) with their subtler reliance on asexual spores. No chaperone was needed for the indoor garden, and even window-boxes (glorified with glass covers and trellises) could be tackled without the need for actually going outdoors. Gardening indoors also had the

LADIES IN BLOOMERS: WOMEN AND THE GARDEN

ABOVE: This rather lewd postcard from c.1910 reminds us of the basic social division between men and vegetables, women and flowers ("greens" was slang for sexual parts).

BELOW: The Wardian case, which allowed ferns and other shade-loving plants to survive smoky atmospheres, was accidentally invented by Dr Nathaniel Bagshaw Ward during his work on breeding moths.

advantage that the pots could be placed on shelves or hung from the roof, so that no uncomfortable bending was needed: as Louisa Johnson reminded her readers in 1840, "Many females are unequal to the fatigue of bending down to flowers and particularly object to the stooping posture." Corsets had a lot to answer for! Where help was needed, the gardener could be invited in, although in larger households helping the mistress of the house was usually a task only the head gardener might be called on to perform and a jobbing gardener would never expect to enter the inner sanctums of the house. Failures (plants, not gardeners) could be easily replaced from the nurserymen who came selling door-to-door. Victorian interiors, with their smoky atmospheres and heavy curtains and fabrics to cut out the light, made raising plants quite difficult, but a wide range of glass cases (based on the Wardian case) and jardinières were available for those who did not have the space or money for a glasshouse.

Soon the fashion spread its wings, and headed out of doors for the comparative liberation of the flower border and even, dare one whisper it, the vegetable plot. As Louisa Johnson argued: "Floriculture ranges itself under the head of female accomplishments in these our days; and we turn with pity from the spirit which will not find in her 'garden of roses' the simplest and purest of pleasures." For most the rose garden was just a start, and if the publications of Jane Loudon are anything to go by, the flower border, bulb borders and even the vegetable plot followed, although as Jane said in her fictional letters

A STOUT ACTIVE GIRL

"I shall speak now of the ornamental shrubs which decorate a flower garden, and which a lady may superintend herself, if her own physical powers are not equal to the fatigue of planting. A labourer or stout active girl may act under her orders."

Louisa Johnson,
Every Lady Her Own Flower Gardener *(1840)*

LEFT: The hand-coloured frontispiece of Louisa Johnson's *Every Lady Her Own Flower Gardener* (1840). The book was a small, pocket-sized manual aimed at the "industrious and economic".

BELOW: Where women went, advertisers followed. Whether it was aprons, gloves, hand cream or soap, the woman that gardened was a woman that bought!

to a lady who had recently moved to the country, "I had not intended saying anything about the kitchen-garden, as it hardly comes within a lady's province."

The fashion for gardening was encouraged by the publication of the first ever gardening books for women (or more correctly "ladies") actually written by women. In 1840, both Jane Loudon and Louisa Johnson published books aimed at the lady gardener. Both envisaged their reading public as the middle-class suburban housewife (or spinster), and both aimed at the novice. However, after that their books diverged. Louisa Johnson's *Every Lady Her Own Flower Gardener* is a small pocket-sized publication of just over 120 pages, aimed, as its author says, at "the industrious and economic" lady who "has a garden but cannot afford a gardener". The tone is slightly melancholic, with hints of disappointments in life which might be ameliorated in the health-giving pleasures of the rose garden. Jane Loudon's *Practical Instructions in Gardening for Ladies* is an encyclopaedic 400 pages, needing a substantial pocket to hold it and covering, with enthusiasm and gusto, everything from grafting to manuring, giving explicit and lengthy instructions on using a spade. Although acknowledging the difficulties that women encountered in their attempts to garden for themselves, Jane Loudon did not let her readers drop by the wayside. Whereas Louisa Johnson acknowledged that ladies might find it inadvisable to venture out in the rain, and awkward to try to bend, Jane Loudon envisages women digging over their own plots, barrowing away the soil, and pruning their own fruit trees. Jane Loudon had been a writer of science fiction before her marriage to garden writer John Claudius Loudon (a man many years older than herself) and something of the rebellious feminist appears to have inhabited her soul – although normally well disguised in her dedication to her husband's career.

By the end of the nineteenth century, there was a rush of garden books written by women who gardened, including the gloriously named *Gardening for the*

RIGHT: The actress and "Gaiety Girl" Marie Studholme models a lawnmower in 1903. In common with modern celebrities, Marie Studholme kept a close control on publicity images, once even suing a dentist for altering a photograph of her without her permission and using it in his advertisements.

BELOW: The combined walking stick and basket was ideal for a lady to collect flowers or do some deadheading. The hook on the stick helped bring long stalks closer.

MISS MARIE STUDHOLME.

Ignorant written by Theresa Earle in 1912, and the self-effacing *The Garden of a Commuter's Wife* (1901) by Mabel Osgood, who lived and gardened in America.

With the advent of the female gardener (be she housewife, woman or "lady") came the perceived need for special tools befitting their more delicate build and refined taste. Whether it was mini-lawnmowers, women's wheelbarrows, lady's spades, flower baskets, flower scissors or aprons, women came to be seen by the manufacturers as a ready market. Lightness was thought to be the absolute key to ladies working in the gardens; as Louisa Johnson stated, "A lady requires peculiar tools for her light work." In 1840 Jane Loudon had recommended that:

> *The first point to be attended to, in order to render the operation of digging less laborious [for a lady], is to provide a suitable spade; that is, one which shall be as light as is consistent with strength, and which will penetrate the ground with the least possible trouble. For this purpose, the blade of what is called a lady's spade is made of not more than half the usual breadth, say not wider than five or six inches, and of smooth polished iron ... The handle is about the usual length, but quite smooth and sufficiently slender for a lady's hand to grasp, and it is*

made of willow, a close smooth and elastic wood, which is tough and tolerably strong, though much lighter than ash, the wood generally used for the handle to gardeners' spades.

These eminently sensible adaptations to the spade meant that even the most delicately built could, with a little practice, turn over at least small spits of earth with confidence. Having turned them, they might want to lift them, and that was where the "lady's wheelbarrow" came into its own. Again, this was a smaller, lighter, version of the usual barrow. Jane Loudon's description of a wheelbarrow was rather less straightforward than that of the spade. "A wheelbarrow," she informed her lady readers, "is a lever of the second kind, in which the weight is carried between the operator, who is the moving power, and the fulcrum, which is represented by the lower part of the wheel."

As well as equipping her readers with spades and wheelbarrows, Jane Loudon also recommended which hoes, rakes and pruning equipment they needed. Of the hoes "the thrust hoe is best adapted for a lady's use, as requiring the least exertion of strength, and being most easily managed," although she admitted that the draw hoe was after all the best tool for making drills or furrows.

The call for specialist ladies' tools was such that, in her 1845 work *The Lady's Country Companion*, Jane Loudon recorded that she had had "numerous applications to know where to procure the gardening implements mentioned". She went on to recommend Messrs Cottan and Hallen, Winsley Street, near Oxford Street, London, who had obviously spotted the gap in the market and promptly filled it.

The rising popularity of lawnmowers in the second half of the nineteenth century created yet another challenge for lady gardeners. Although at first seen as ideal exercise for the gentleman of the house (or his gardener), it was not long before especially small lawnmowers were being created that might be pushed by the eager female gardener, or even by a child. Still heavy in comparison with modern mowers, the machine's width was reduced so that it could just about be pushed by an eager female, although it might take all day to mow a small lawn.

From the early days, lawnmower manufacturers started to use images of women pushing their products as evidence of how light and easy the machines were, regardless of whether they expected women to use them or not. Immaculately dressed in the fashions of the times, women have been used to advertise everything from Ransomes Victorian iron mowers to 1970s Hover Mowers and modern "ride-on-mowers".

Gardening as a career was not an option open to women in the male-oriented world of the Victorian garden. Training to become a professional gardener was largely carried out on the job, with the male gardeners living in for the long years, as they graduated from garden boy to head gardener. Women were not allowed to join their ranks. It was not until the very end of the nineteenth century that the first gardening schools for women were set up to allow them to by-pass the bothy and yet still become professional

ABOVE TOP: The advent of petrol-driven mowers should have allowed more women to use even the large machines with little effort, but attaching an engine to a mower often put women off. The tie and trousers in this photograph may suggest that it was taken at a gardening school for women.

ABOVE: Hover mowers really did "float", and all the main manufacturers used women in their advertising to prove how light they really were.

gardeners. In 1891, the Horticultural College at Swanley, Kent, let in its first female students, at first in a mixed class but soon as a female-only one. Even so, the college principal (Mr Propert) declared that gardening work was undesirable "in every way" for women, who might lose their proper womanly shape and develop masculine muscles. In 1898, the University of Reading (Berkshire) opened its famous Lady Warwick Hostel, sponsored by Daisy, Lady Warwick. The Lady Warwick school eventually became the successful Studley Castle Horticultural and Agricultural College for Women, based at Studley in Warwickshire. At the other end of the country, Frances Wolseley, daughter of Field Marshal Garnet Wolseley, 1st Viscount Wolseley, was busy setting up her own gardening school at Glynde, their country home in Sussex. The idea for the Glynde school appears to have its origin with her mother hiring a female gardener who had been deserted by her husband and left with children to support. It struck Frances that gardening, which she herself enjoyed as a hobby, would be an excellent profession for well-educated and intelligent women. These newly trained lady gardeners would in turn (in Frances's words) become "artistic, well-educated, refined, head gardeners", "lending intelligence, good taste [and] refinement towards securing better cultivation of our great country".

Studley, Swanley and Glynde were at the vanguard of gardening schools for women. In the years between 1899 and 1922, at least 22 private schools were set up to train lady gardeners. Bearing a strong resemblance to small-scale boarding or finishing schools, most took just a handful of women a year, usually starting them at the age of 18 or 20. Courses lasted one or two years and equipped the women to become head gardeners in smaller establishments,

A LIFE OF ONE'S OWN

"The existence of women who, whether they like it or not are bound to work for their livelihoods, is as a rule, only unwillingly recognized as an exception; the existence of women who claim to have a life of their own is still more upsetting to all ideas of a well-constituted universe."

Mrs Louise Creighton, President of the Union of Women Workers (1895–97)

Studley Castle Horticultural College for Women. A lesson in Pruning.

LADIES IN BLOOMERS — WOMEN AND THE GARDEN

or to set up on their own as jobbing gardeners or market gardeners. Those who had less confidence (or less monetary backing) could become "companion gardeners", living-in with a spinster or widow and providing social as well as horticultural companionship, or teach nature studies and gardening to children. The aim of the schools, as set out by Frances Wolseley, was not to supplant clever, able, male gardeners, but to complement them, bringing the gentle artistic touch of a woman into England's gardens. In fact, it was not just England that was to be so enriched – several schools had training for women who wished to garden in the colonies, mostly as overseers in market gardens or in small gardens for English families abroad. Frances Wolseley thought that such a career held out "decidedly good prospects" to the right sort of woman, one who could face a degree of danger and did not mind the difficulties presented by having to garden in cholera belt and veil (the latter a protection against sand storms).

The question of what to wear exercised the minds of even those lady gardeners who chose to stay in England. Prior to the First World War, all the schools had gardening uniforms of full-length dresses, or long skirts with blouses and ties, and straw bonnets or hats. Aprons, gloves and skirts worn whilst at work were made slightly more waterproof with the aid of oilcloth around the hems. The ladies who trained at Kew Gardens in 1901 were issued with bloomers and spats, but were requested to wear full-length coats over their bloomers while in the public gaze. The outbreak of war and the consequent increase in women working led to a relaxation of dress code for manual workers, and "airmen's" trousers or bloomers became the accepted norm.

OPPOSITE ABOVE: Whether through lack of lawn size or lack of lawnmower (or lack of man to push lawnmower), this women has resorted to shears!

OPPOSITE BELOW: Many of the tutors at early women's gardening schools were men. Here the women at Studley Horticultural College are given a lesson in pruning wall fruits.

ABOVE: By 1916 uniforms had become more practical, with long boots, leggings and "aviation skirts". These girls at Glynde School also wore blouses, ties and hessian aprons. The uniform at Glynde was khaki in colour, as the soil was a pale colour and would show up too much on a dark uniform.

DOING THEIR BIT

A Gardener and a Baker of the Women's Auxiliary Army Corps

RIGHT: The two world wars made the sight of females in the workplace a more familiar one.

Waterperry (Oxfordshire) was one of the most famous schools for women, with its equally famous principal Beatrix Havergal. Beatrix herself had trained at the Thatcham School, and then, with her partner Avice Saunders, set up the Pusey School for Lady Gardeners in 1927. This was so successful that by the outbreak of the Second World War, they had taken over an old manor house at Waterperry owned by Magdalen College, Oxford, to allow numbers to expand. Waterperry became so famous that years after its eventual demise, advertisements for female gardeners still optimistically asked for candidates with a Waterperry diploma. Amongst the many famous gardeners that passed

 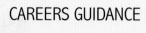

IN THE SPRING.

We are getting busy in the Garden.

through Waterperry were Pamela Schwerdt and Sibylle Kreutzberger, who went on to work for Vita Sackville-West in her gardens at Sissinghurst.

The outbreak of the First World War revolutionized attitudes to women's roles in horticulture and agriculture. Where once only the wives of labourers had helped with the harvest or grown their own herbs and vegetables, now middle- and even upper-class women were expected to join in and the Women's National Land Service Corps (later integrated into the Women's Land Army) oversaw the placement of women gardeners throughout the country, making up for men sent to

Good Gardening

Edited by H·H·Thomas

6d

AUGUST
·1937·

LADIES IN BLOOMERS: WOMEN AND THE GARDEN

GARDENING
FOR ALL

6D

ALDINE HANDY SERIES

OPPOSITE: Almost as difficult to garden in as the Victorian long dress and corset, this hat was the epitome of fashionable gardening in the inter-war period!

LEFT: This inter-war publication showed the ideal family, with mother tending the sweet-peas and father digging the cabbage patch.

war. When peace came again, the sight of middle-class women wielding a hoe or a fork was no longer as shocking as it had been in Victorian times. The growth of the inter-war suburbs, owned by families who could not aspire to a full-time gardener, gave opportunities for women to join in with the care of the garden. Although women were still associated with flower borders and not expected to meddle with the "veg", at least they had broken free of the fern house and conservatory.

The Second World War, and the Dig for Victory campaign, again saw women on the "Garden Front" and the government encouraged women to take on allotments of their own (*see* Chapter 7). The Women's Institute even ran schemes for groups of women to take on allotments which had been abandoned by men when they were called up. The gardening press was full of reports of elderly grandmothers running several plots single-handedly as an example to the nation, and magazines such as *Woman* ran advice columns which combined "In the Kitchen" with "In the Garden". This time, the impact was longer lasting. Although some women retreated again to the flower beds, for others the vegetable plot and the horticultural show became a lifelong habit.

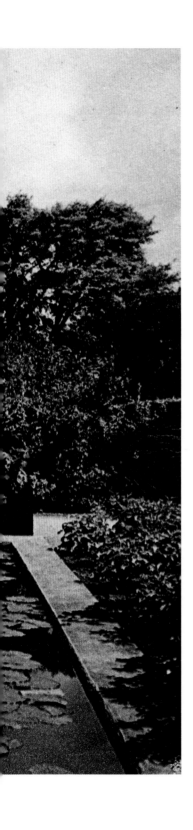

6

The Inter-war
Years:
New Homes,
New Gardens

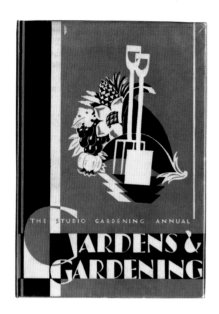

"Homes Fit for Heroes" was the rallying cry of the housing movement that followed the end of the First World War. In the campaign that followed, over four million new houses were built, including the first ever council housing. As semi-detached suburbia spread across the nation in the 1920s and '30s, semi-detached gardens followed, each with their small, neat, front garden and long, thin rear plot. Housing Acts of 1919 and 1930 defined the new pattern by setting maximum densities at 12 houses per acre. Cul-de-sacs, a favourite of the suburban planners, created ideal conditions for gardens to thrive along quiet streets, still devoid of cars and endless dropped kerb entrances. The Tudorbethan and Tyrolean styles were the favourites for private developments, with three-bedroom properties costing £500–600 in the London suburbs of the 1930s. Detached houses, often built at only eight houses an acre, cost as little as £650 if one was prepared to move slightly further out of town. For those who could not bear to be further than six miles (10 kilometres) from Regent's Park, the Woodside Park estate in Finchley provided three-bedroom detached properties with integral garage for only £1,195 (in weekly repayment instalments of 25s 8d). The low density of housing allowed large rear gardens, in many cases similar to the size of a traditional allotment – 27 feet (8.25 metres) wide by 90–100 feet (27–30 metres) long – no coincidence when the nation had recently had to deal with a sea blockade that had aimed to starve it into submission. In the idyllic inter-war years, these gardens were filled with roses and rock gardens in the calm after the storm, and before the next one broke.

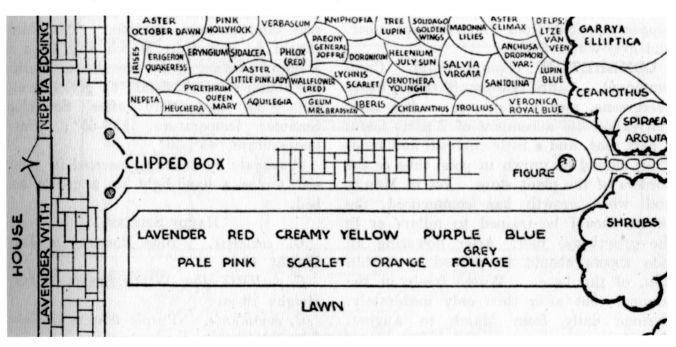

HUMOROUS NEIGHBOUR (to Amateur Gardener "Crazy" paving his garden)— "Hullo, Browne, Gone Jig-saw Crazy?"

LEFT: The inter-war fad for crazy paving goes truly crazy in this cartoon. This type of paving was usually more muted in colour, relying for its effect on shapes rather than tones.

BELOW: In 1938 Wills's cigarette cards featured 50 hints on gardening for the amateur. First among these were instructions on laying paving, neatening edges and creating a sunken (paved) lily pond.

Paving, paving and more paving was the gardener's mantra in the 1930s. As concrete paving became cheaper, so it became the fashion for the garden to include areas devoted to the art of the amateur paver. Paving made a garden tidy, and the 1930s suburban garden prided itself on tidiness. Paving could either be laid in its original slabs or, for the latest fashion, it could be broken up and re-laid as crazy paving, a fashion which supposedly originated in Ancient Rome. Gardening books were full of instructions and diagrams on how to lay crazy paving (starting with the breaking up of the slabs), and many a suburban gardener made good use of the opportunity to get rid of some old garden and household rubble by using it as a foundation for the path. For the really adventurous gardener, coloured cement was available so that the pieces of paving could be bedded in a red or blue surround. In addition to paths, the edges of flowerbeds could be paved to prevent ugly bare patches in lawns when flowers flopped over onto the grass – actually a suggestion also championed by garden designer Gertrude Jekyll on a somewhat grander scale. Garden seats could be placed on a snug surround of concrete, kept weed-free and guaranteed not to have any messy wear marks from heels dangling from the seat. Sundials and bird baths (also a favourite of the do-it-yourself concrete gardener) could be set on a plinth of paving, and lily ponds made of concrete could be sunken and stepped, yet again using paving. With the new fashion for light in the house and the mingling of outdoor and indoor through the use of "French windows" and the revolutionary sliding doors, many 1930s houses also provided ideal opportunities for creating a small paved terrace or patio immediately adjacent to the living room.

MAKING A WATER-LILY POOL (B)

CONCRETE CRAZY PAVING

Perennials for the Rockery

BY APPOINTMENT
TO HER MAJESTY THE QUEEN
SEEDSMEN

"IDEAL"
COLLECTION OF
PERENNIALS
FOR THE
ROCKERY
(6 Choice Varieties)

Carters
TESTED SEEDS

RAYNES PARK,
LONDON, S.W. 20.

ABOVE: Rockeries were so popular in the inter-war garden that several seed suppliers produced mixed collections specifically for them.

Whatever was not paved could be rocked! Rock gardens had been popular since the Victorian period, with larger gardens aspiring to entire alpine ranges. But the 1930s saw the widespread adoption of the smaller suburban rockery, planted with small, neat plants. Carters' nursery sold specific rock-garden collections which included *Alyssum saxatile compactum* (yellow), aubretia hybrids (various colours), *Arabis alpina* (white rock cress), *Campanula carpatica*, *Dianthus deltoides* (a bright pink "pink") and *Iberis gibraltarica*. Other popular plants for the 1930s rock garden included various saxifrages, *Anemone apennina* (windflower), alpine campanulas (bellflower), gentians, dwarf phlox, *Linaria alpina* (toadflax) and the various ericas (heathers). Alexander Edwards, curator of the rock garden at the Royal Botanic Gardens, Kew, listed plants suitable not only for the rock garden but also the alpine house (a cool glasshouse), scree gardens, rocky bog gardens, marsh gardens, paved gardens and wall gardens. Within these, one could choose from bulbs, annuals, perennials, plants for shady sites, plants for sunny sites, peat-loving plants, creeping plants, trailing plants, lime lovers and lime haters, ferns, shrubs and even trees for the rockery. Whatever shape or form your garden took, there was a rockery and rock plant for you.

Wall gardens were extremely popular in the 1920s and '30s, offering a solution not only to sloping gardens which could be terraced but also to small gardens where a rock wall would create more planting space. In the words of Edwards, "The wall [garden] will enable the owner of a small garden, where there is no room for a larger rock garden on orthodox lines, to grow the ever popular alpines and rock plants." Wall gardens housed many of the same varieties of plants that the rockery did, but with the addition of trailing plants and ferns. Gertrude Jekyll recommended the silvery leaf saxifrages or the fragrant dianthus and devoted whole books to wall, water and woodland gardens.

In the space that was left between the rockery, the wall-terrace and the paving, fashionable gardeners inserted a paved lily pond, lawn and flower borders. Water-lily ponds were particularly prized, giving the opportunity to show off the hybrid water lilies which had been developed by nurseries such as Latour-Marliac (in south-west France) in the 1890s and early 1900s and were now within the reach of the more modest gardener. Set within the immaculately striped lawn, the waters sparkled in their nest of crazy paving.

Colour was the key to the flower borders, with clumps or drifts of perennial plants being used as a base and annuals added as needs be. In his popular 1930s work *New Illustrated Gardening Encyclopaedia*, Richard Sudell wrote that:

Colour schemes for the herbaceous borders will vary according to taste, but a few suggestions might be helpful. Try a blue, mauve and white border with occasional groups of shell pink; or blue and yellow. Start with pale shades, increase to bright and back again to pale tints; start with pinks, whites and reds, increase to blues, yellows and orange and back to pinks and reds; for grouping try Salvia virgata nemerosa *(purple) with* Helenium July Sun *(Orange); Lavender with* Nepeta mussini*; deep blue Delphiniums with white Madonna Lilies; Cheiranthus (deep orange) with* Viola cornuta *or royal blue Forget-me-nots.*

Front gardens were often formal as befitted their small size in the suburban semi-detached, with a paved path, narrow borders (often with standard roses), a handkerchief of lawn and a central sundial or birdbath. The 1930s front garden was not a place to flaunt any unconventionality.

If the suburban garden was often defined by its crazy paving and startlingly vibrant lupins, the upper-class garden of the 1920s and '30s could be a riot of

LEFT: Cracks between paving slabs could either be filled with cement (in a range of colours!) or planted up with a selection of scree-loving plants as here.

ABOVE: Wall gardens and crazy paving were fashionable even in the most tasteful of garden — here illustrating the 1935 catalogue for Dartington Hall gardens, in Devon.

softness and romance, thanks to designers such as Norah Lindsay. Norah Mary Madeline Lindsay (née Bourke) was born in colonial India in 1873, one of several women of the Victorian era who were to define gardens of the 1920s and '30s (Gertrude Jekyll and Vita Sackville-West being others). Emma Bourke, Norah's mother, was an acknowledged beauty who had caught the eye (and heart) of the Prince of Wales, later Edward VII. The family moved easily in the social circles on the edge of the court and at the heart of the political and artistic elite and, after her marriage to Harry Lindsay, Norah kept up the social whirl at country-house weekends amongst the Churchills, Astors and Cunards

🌿 THE INTER-WAR YEARS: NEW HOMES, NEW GARDENS

and alongside other gardening practitioners such as Lady Ottoline Morrell, Edith Wharton and Ellen Willmott. Her own home at Sutton Courtenay (Oxfordshire) was the first triumph of her garden art. Here, she developed her style of informal flower borders contrasted with topiary and clipped hedging, the geometric contrasting with overflowing abundance. She published her garden articles in *Country Life*, *Vogue's House and Garden Book* and even started a book herself called *Garden Idyll* (never completed). Plants with long flowering seasons, well-prepared soil and a planting scheme of *ton sur ton* (tone on tone) were the keys to Norah's success. Long borders, old-fashioned scented roses, wide paths and dark yew hedging were her foundations: "Above all, let no earth be visible, but crowd up the front with large comfortable mats of permanent things, which can brim over the edge in uneven groups." After the failure of her marriage and the collapse of her finances, Norah Lindsay made a career out of a necessity and combined her social life with hard work in the gardens of the houses she visited. The effect of "thoughtless abundance", actually obtained by skilful planting and outlay of vast sums of money, appealed to the country-house set, and through the 1920s and '30s Norah designed gardens at Cliveden (for the Astors), Blickling Hall (for Philip Kerr), Kelmarsh Hall and Ditchley Park (for Ronnie and Nancy Tree – later Nancy Lancaster), and Fort Belvedere for the then Prince of Wales. Perhaps her most important garden connection was with Lawrence (Johnny) Johnston, whose gardens at Hidcote (Gloucestershire) and La Serre de la Madone (France) were to become second homes for her.

Famous for its mix of formal and informal, rare plants and garden "rooms", Hidcote has become for many the epitome of the 1930s gardens style. Lawrence Johnston first came to Hidcote in 1907, with his mother. It was she who commenced the gardens there, but it was Lawrence who was to bring them to their full glory. Johnston was a plant lover rather than a designer; he went on plant-hunting expeditions to South America, South Africa and the Near East. He laid out axial lines and a structure redolent of his beloved Italy, where he also gardened. "Rooms" leading off from those axes contained pools or grass walks, hornbeam "avenues" and masses of silvery foliage and roses. Wilder areas housed plants collected from jungle areas, replete with trickling water weaving through dripping foliage, although his love of the exotic was tamed by the Gloucestershire climate and wilder planting was reserved for his "Hidcote of

BELOW: Advances in cement and concrete manufacture meant that a range of features could be made to suit most pockets. Cement manufacturers saw the garden as a new market for them. Lily ponds, of all sizes, were typically shallow with apsidal ends, giving a hint of the Continent.

ABOVE: This grand expanse of paving and water was part of William Wood's exhibition garden at Chelsea Horticultural Show in 1934.

the South", as he called his gardens at La Serre de la Madone, near Menton in the South of France. The mix of romantic and severe, structured yet exuberant became the hallmark of the English garden style. Seen at its best in gardens such as Sissinghurst (Kent), it also typifies Arts and Crafts gardens such as Rodmarton (Gloucestershire) and even the original design of Great Dixter (Sussex) – the latter enhanced by the more recent plantings of Christopher Lloyd but originally laid out by his father, Nathaniel Lloyd, in the 1920s and '30s.

Great Dixter was in many ways the classic partnership garden, with Nathaniel Lloyd providing much of the structure, the sunken garden planting and the famous topiary pieces, whilst his wife Daisy contributed the wilder meadow areas. The redesigned house and the hard landscaping of the garden were by the architect Lutyens, and even the modern garden owes much to its original Lutyens framework – bringing the Edwardian into the modern. Sissinghurst Castle, on the other hand, attracted Vita Sackville-West and her husband Harold Nicolson for its Tudor roots, onto which they grafted the

THE INTER-WAR YEARS: NEW HOMES, NEW GARDENS

perfect English garden. Again, the structure of garden rooms allows an informal heart to beat within a formal skeleton. It was Nicolson who was responsible for the structure and what Vita referred to as the "strong lines", while she filled the garden with romance and roses.

> *Gardens should be romantic but severe,*
> *Strike your strong lines, and take no further care*
> *Of such extravagance as pours the rose*
> *In wind-blown fountains down the broken walls.*
> Vita Sackville-West – "The Garden"

Sissinghurst was not the only garden made by Vita and her husband; from 1915 until 1930 they had cut their gardening teeth at Long Barn, near Vita's beloved Knole in Sevenoaks. But over a period of 32 years, they made

BELOW: Statuesque lupins were a popular component of the flower border, providing a colour range of mauves, pinks, salmons and oranges. George Russell of York (shown here) was responsible for the breeding of the famous strain of Russell lupins, many of which were lost to virus in the 1950s.

Bakers
SEEDS 1939

ABOVE: Russell's lupins came in nearly all the colours of the rainbow!

BELOW: The red borders at Hidcote (1960s). Single-colour gardens and borders were becoming popular from the 1930s onwards. Sissinghurst had its white garden and Hidcote its red borders.

OPPOSITE: Vita Sackville-West on the steps of the famous tower at Sissinghurst, with her dog Rollo.

Sissinghurst and the views from its ancient towers one of the most famous gardens in the world. Already open to the public during Vita's life, it passed to the National Trust on her death, joining Hidcote under its care. What the gardens of Lawrence Johnston, Norah Lindsay and Vita Sackville-West have in common is not just their design style but the knowledgeable plantsmanship of the people who created them. To the visitor, the abundance appears (as Norah Lindsay would have claimed) "laissez faire", the plants crowding in amongst their retaining hedges and ancient manor-house walls, but the complementary colours and heights and the perpetual display through the seasons are all hallmarks of the plantsperson at work. Each employed gardeners to fulfil their artistic visions, but each had intimate knowledge of the tools with which they worked.

Romance in the rose garden was not to all tastes, and echoing the neat exactitude of the suburban paved garden came the "'progressive garden" as promoted by *The Studio Gardening Annual* of 1932. With contributions by Percy Izzard and J. Bowater Vernon, *The Studio* tackled town gardens and the "modern" garden, and featured designs by up-and-coming architects such as Geoffrey Jellicoe, Percy Cane and the landscape company of Vernon Bros. Reinforced concrete made an appearance here, as did paving and sunken pools. The inspiration for small courtyard gardens was the Pompeii style, with water spouting from masks inset into walls, sculpture in relief, and stone or wood pergolas. The same style could be applied to courtyard or roof gardens, with even the smallest Belgravia basement looking out onto a perfect classical scene. Vernon Bros even took the Roman garden altar as an inspiration for its wealthy clients, many of whom would have visited Pompeii itself, where the houses were being excavated through the inter-war period.

Roof gardens were a new fashion in England in the 1930s, following rather late in the footsteps of Paris and New York, where wealthy apartment-dwellers had long been able to saunter out for an evening under the stars. Fountains and pools were popular, with reportedly no difficulty being experienced with weight, although it was recommended that building strengths be tested first if large amounts of paving were to be installed. The architectural fashion for flat roofs meant that many of the newer buildings were made with a garden design as integral. Larger office blocks allowed space for lawns and trees, and there was

THE INTER-WAR YEARS: NEW HOMES, NEW GARDENS

ABOVE: A view down one of the axial paths at Sutton Courtenay, the home of Norah Lindsay.

BELOW RIGHT: This 1950s guide to the Derry and Toms roof garden pictures the woodland area and stream. The gardens continued to open through the store's change of hands (to Biba) and are still open by prior arrangement.

even a nine-hole golf-putting course and a rock garden on the roof of Adelaide House (near London Bridge). Several shops joined in the fashion, the most famous being the gardens on the roof at Selfridges in Oxford Street and Derry and Toms in High Street Kensington. The garden at Selfridges was coolly modernist, with large areas of paving and flower beds raised in concrete-blocked low walls. The Derry and Toms Garden covered 1.5 acres (0.6 hectares) and had zoned areas with themed gardens, including a woodland water garden (replete with ducks and grassy banks), a Spanish (or Moorish) garden with palms and fountains and even a campanile, and a Tudor garden with a pathway of herringbone brickwork and arches. With the aid of artesian wells in the basement areas of the shop, and a 36-inch (90-centimetre) layer of topsoil all hoisted up to 100 feet (30 metres) above pavement level, the gardens opened in 1938 with over 500 varieties of plants in them. The gardens were an enormous success, with

THE Derry ROOF GARDENS

"A country retreat beneath a myriad shoppers feet"

Derry and Toms, Kensington High Street, London, W.8 : WEStern 8181

THE INTER-WAR YEARS: NEW HOMES, NEW GARDENS

visitors including the royal family, and a visitors' book was kept with signatures from stars of stage and screen. More humble visitors were charged a shilling to visit. Over the following 30 years, more than £120,000 was raised from the entrance fees and donated to local charities. The gardens were taken on by Biba when the store changed hands, and some alterations took place, but recent restorations under the present owner (Richard Branson) have seen the gardens open again in all their 1930s glory, although the distant views of the green Surrey hills are no more!

Roof gardens, with their frequent use of paving and raised ponds, echoed the modernist style hinted at in many suburban gardens. One of the foremost proponents of this style was the designer Percy Cane. Essex-born, Percy Cane's first job was with the famous metal-window manufacturers Crittall – themselves a distinctive hallmark of so many inter-war windows and founders of the "model village" for their employees at the Silver End factory site. Inspired by the gardens designed by Harold Peto at Easton Lodge, Cane trained at the horticultural college in Chelmsford. His own style was a mix of rock and water gardens (often in the Japanese spirit), flagstones and courtyards, cherry trees and rose gardens. Working in large gardens, he introduced "glades" with paths wending through ornamental trees. One of his best-known gardens was that at Dartington Hall (Devon), by then an influential arts centre as well as a nursery and supplier of plants and trees. Perhaps less well known now outside his

BELOW: The Derry and Toms Spanish garden, complete with campanile and palms.

ABOVE: The roof gardens at Selfridges. Not as extensive as Derry and Toms, it was more modernist in style.

BELOW: Writer, cat lover and gardener, Beverley Nichols, whose gently wry books have outlasted the several gardens that he created.

native Essex, Percy Cane was awarded eight gold and three silver-gilt medals at Chelsea Flower Show between 1921 and 1953, as well as the prestigious RHS Veitch medal. His work was feted in the popular *My Garden, Illustrated*, which he wrote for and edited from 1918, and his designs inspired many a suburban gardener, whether they knew it or not.

Catering for the ever-booming interest in gardens came a whole host of gardening books and periodicals – from the strictly instructional via the aspirational to the plain chatty. Books on "how I did my garden" were increasingly popular, including Francis Hadfield Farthing's *Every Day in My Garden* (1929), Alfred Harrison's *How We Made Our Garden* (1935) and *My Town Garden* by Lady Seton (1927). The scene for these outpourings had been set in the pre-war period, but now they emerged fully fledged with a mixture of musings on plants and people. The "little book" (as it called itself) *My Garden* was perhaps the most successful of these. A monthly publication of some 100-plus pages, it featured a mix of usually undemanding articles, often by owners of substantial gardens in a style which lived up to its full title of *My Garden: An Intimate Magazine for Garden Lovers*. Articles start with sentences such as "We were faced with the perpetual problem of a wet lawn" or promise to help solve the problems of labour shortage. Discrete advertisements for tennis courts, teak garden furniture and life assurance for those "past middle age" combine with snatches of poetry and prose. One of its earliest contributors was the

ABOVE: This sunlit painting by Guy Lipscombe captures the golden atmosphere of gardens between the wars.

author Beverley Nichols, whose gently self-mocking and severely misogynistic gardening "autobiographies" were hallmarks of the 1930s. *Down the Garden Path*, the first in his trilogy about the cottage and garden at "Allways" (his cottage at Glatton, Huntingdonshire), was a best-seller which ran for 32 editions and has rarely been out of print – a testimony to the enthusiasm for that idyllic garden life of the inter-war period. In the first of his articles for *My*

Garden, Nichols drew on a similarly popular author – E.F. Benson and his well-known character, the extremely snobbish Lucia – for a description of another 1930s phenomenon, the theme garden. Whether a Shakespeare garden (as with Lucia), a poetry garden or a friendship garden (perhaps the most difficult, as it was composed of a random selection of plants given by friends), small sentimental borders were the final touch for many an inter-war garden. Nichols himself laid claim to a "thieves' garden" – constructed from cuttings and rootings of plants filched from other gardens open to the public, only to have to retract in the next edition of *My Garden*, after Kew had written in horrified indignation that some of its own rare collection had apparently found its way to Nichols's garden! The author immediately apologized, stating that the piece had been written lightheartedly in "a spirit of whimsical fooling", which summed up perfectly much of his writing.

ABOVE: An idyllic summerhouse from the Dartington Hall collection.

BELOW: The Pyghtle Works were well known for their Arts and Crafts style garden furniture. They also made church furnishings.

In 1927, the country finally confessed that it really was a "nation of gardeners" with the launch of the National Gardens Scheme (NGS), now popularly known as the "Yellow Book" scheme from its distinctive publication. In that first year, 609 private gardens opened their gates to the public in aid

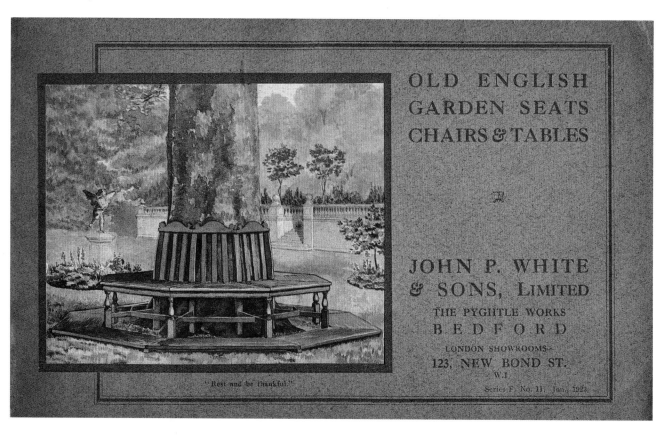

OLD ENGLISH
GARDEN SEATS
CHAIRS & TABLES

JOHN P. WHITE
& SONS, LIMITED
THE PYGHTLE WORKS
BEDFORD
LONDON SHOWROOMS
123, NEW BOND ST.
W.I
Series F. No. 11. Jan. 1923.

"Rest and be thankful."

THE INTER-WAR YEARS: NEW HOMES, NEW GARDENS

THE GARDENS OF ENGLAND AND WALES

OPEN TO THE PUBLIC IN AID OF THE QUEEN'S
INSTITUTE OF DISTRICT NURSING

Classified by dates and alphabetically

Illustrated Edition. Preface by
CHRISTOPHER HUSSEY

1934

Published for
The Queen's Institute of District Nursing
57 Lower Belgrave Street, London, S.W.1
by
Country Life Ltd., 20 Tavistock Street, London, W.C.2

ONE SHILLING

LEFT: Later known as the Yellow Book, the National Gardens Scheme list of gardens open to the public did not take on its distinctive yellow covering until the 1950s.

of the nurses of the Queen's Nursing Institute. It was only four years later that the first "Yellow Book" appeared, with over 1,000 gardens, although until the 1950s it was actually a variety of pastel shades. In the post-war period, the NGS combined with the National Trust to highlight the need for important gardens to be preserved and accessible. Blickling was the first major country house taken on by the National Trust, in 1940, and many more followed during the immediate post-war period. Hidcote in Gloucestershire was the first garden acquired in its own right by the Trust, in 1948. Prior to that, the Trust had concentrated on natural landscapes, with country houses (and their gardens) incidental. For many years, the entrance fee to gardens was held at a shilling, giving rise to Vita Sackville-West's nickname of "the shillingses" for visitors at her own garden at Sissinghurst.

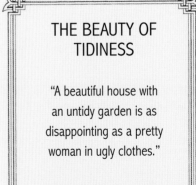

THE BEAUTY OF TIDINESS

"A beautiful house with an untidy garden is as disappointing as a pretty woman in ugly clothes."

My Garden: An Intimate Magazine for Garden Lovers, *January 1934*

7

Allotment
Fever

"With spades and hoes and ploughs, stand up now, stand up now. Your freedom to uphold ..." So ran the rallying call of the first men to fight for the right for a plot to cultivate. In the seventeenth century, Gerrard Winstanley founded a movement called "the True Levellers", known by their opponents as "the Diggers". The True Levellers believed that no man should own land or property, but that each should have a share according to their needs. In 1649, Winstanley led his followers onto "waste" and common lands in Surrey, where they cultivated crops free of restrictions and rents. Alas for Winstanley, the local landowners did not take kindly to his trespass or to his gifts of food to the poor, and the Diggers were evicted. Despite their failure, the Digger movement remained a rallying cry for those who fought enclosure and privatization of land into the twentieth century.

Although Winstanley wildly overestimated the zeal for social reform of Oliver Cromwell, and he eventually failed to establish his Digger community, he did correctly identify the social divide that enclosure of the land represented. In his *A Declaration from the Poor Oppressed People of England*, he accused the landowners of theft, saying that: "The power of enclosing land and owning property was brought into the creation by your ancestors by the sword; which first did murder their fellow creatures, men, and after plunder or steal away their land, and left this land successively to you, their children. And therefore, though you did not kill or thieve, yet you hold that cursed thing in your hand

by the power of the sword." If Winstanley could have foreseen the great swing towards "parliamentary" field enclosure in the subsequent centuries, he might have dug his community in a little deeper and hoed just that little bit harder.

By the late eighteenth and early nineteenth centuries, the great "agricultural improvers" of the period had decided that the way to greater efficiency and increased profits – for the landholders – lay in the privatization and enclosure of the "open field system". This age-old system, in which the land of a parish or manor was divided into three or four large fields, each with a complex system of strips and furlongs rented and ploughed by individuals, sometimes allotted in their hundreds, was held by those improvers to be inefficient and backward-looking. Whether or not they were right, what the system did allow was for each household – except the very poorest – to have its own strip of rented land for crops, its own headland to graze a cow, and its own rights of common for wood and pasture. With enclosure, all that was taken away. Labourers truly became wage slaves and the garden of England was fenced in – with them on the outside.

With the poverty of the English labourer becoming a by-word around Europe, and tax for the provision of poor relief rocketing, allotments were to be the saving of a nation divided. The New Poor Law of 1834 may well have acted as a momentum for allotment provision, with over 50 sites established in that year alone, a substantial increase on the trickle of sites in the late eighteenth century. In contrast, during the entire period between c.1795 and c.1830 only 87 allotment

> "It may not be easy to define what an allotment is, but it is like an elephant, you recognize it when you see it."
> *Mr R. Hudson (Minister of Agriculture)*
> *August 1943*

> An allotment is defined as "an area of land not exceeding 40 poles in extent which is wholly or mainly cultivated by the occupier who rents the land for the production of vegetables or fruit crops for consumption by himself and his family."
> *Allotment Act 1922*

ABOVE: This plot boasts a rather up-market summerhouse or shed, and may in fact be a "guinea garden" rather than an allotment.

BELOW: By the nineteenth century rhubarb had become a popular fruit, along with gooseberries.

ALLOTMENTS.

We do honour to the first man
Who raised a stick of Rhubarb.

sites (sites rather than plots) have been identified. At first only cautiously adopted as a philanthropic measure in a few parishes, "experiments" quickly showed that the provision of small parcels of land for rent to agricultural labourers gave back not only their dinner but their dignity. Soon, elaborate schemes were being tried out to give deserving tenants a "cot and cow", a pig, or parcels of land up to a quarter of an acre (a tenth of a hectare). Some generous schemes resulted in labourers setting up in market gardening, a move which upset the tenant farmers who relied on willing labour and captive food markets. Some landholders claimed that such schemes would result in the men becoming lazy at work, marrying too early (with the confidence of being able to provide for their family come what may), and the consequent birth of "too many children".

Many allotments came at a price, however – that of social blackmail. Complex rules and regulations demanded of the allotment holders attendance at church, absence from the ale house and a character of "sobriety and morality". Hard work for the master, regardless of competing needs down on the allotment, were to be combined with due attendance to "the spiritual work" demanded by the Heavenly Master on a Sunday. Allotments, lectured the vicar of Tysoe (Warwickshire), were only suited to a man if he could prove sufficient leisure time to work them, a capacity for hard work undiminished by competing demands, and an upright character. In fact many labourers found their allotments something of a burden, although a necessary one. An investigator from the *Daily News* recorded one nineteenth-century Oxford labourer as saying, "I sometimes think I likes the winter better nor [than] summer. In winter, when you done your work, you can go 'ome and rest a' ha' a bit o' comfort. But in the summer you has to do yer day's work and then go on the allotment."

Early allotments had a chequered life, few being protected from sale by the landowner. Rents varied widely, with much higher rents on urban sites despite

ALLOTMENT FEVER

these plots often being slightly smaller, perhaps a response to the higher price of town land or more active farm labourers being willing to take on larger plots. Individual landholders also had enormous influence on the provision of allotments in particular regions. Lord Braybrooke, for example, established allotments in Saffron Walden and Littlebury as part of his estate at Audley End (Essex), and promoted allotments across north Essex and south Cambridgeshire.

The campaign for allotments was taken up by the eloquently named Society for Bettering the Condition and Increasing the Comforts of the Poor (founded in 1796) and the Labourers' Friend Society (which first met in 1832). Despite refusal to make allotment provision compulsory in acts of 1819, 1831 and 1887,

BELOW LEFT: This "popular annual for amateur allotment holders and working gardeners" portrays an idyllic rural image with bees and even cows hinted at down on the plot.

BELOW: The National Allotment and Gardens Society was founded in 1901 and has continued to promote and help safeguard allotments to the present day under the title National Society of Allotment and Leisure Gardeners.

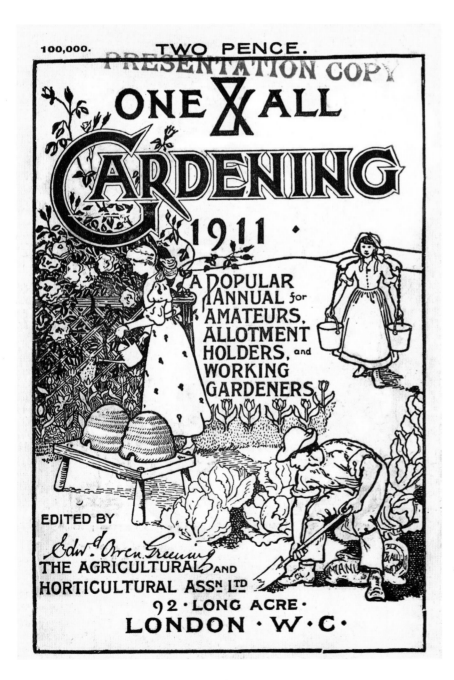

the day of allotments dawned finally in 1889. The Representation of the People Act of 1884 had extended the franchise to include male agricultural labourers, and the county council elections of 1889 were nicknamed the "allotment elections", with councillors being voted in or out by the newly enfranchised depending on their standing on allotments. In Spalding (Lincolnshire), Halley Stewart stood for the Liberals on the "allotment ticket" and, having won the seat, retained it for the next seven years. Overall, the "allotment party" won by a small majority and by 1890 there were just over 440,000 allotments, spreading for the first time into the urban areas. A Local Government Act in 1894 gave further powers for both voluntary and compulsory creation of allotments, whilst those authorities that were still dragging their heels were addressed by the Smallholdings and Allotments Act of 1908, which forced the county councils to become proactive and ascertain what land was required for allotments. Even then, not all councils or parishes were equally enthusiastic and there were major differences between east and west, urban and rural.

Many railway companies rented allotment land to their employees, and rail passengers could while away many an hour watching people tending their allotment plots on the slopes of the embankments, until health and safety brought the sight to an end. Factory workers, then often based in small manufactories in the rural areas, also took up allotments. Indeed, the only members of society who did not seem to embrace the joys of allotment digging were the aristocracy and professionals, such as vets, doctors and clergymen, who seem to have stood aloof, at least in the rural areas. Some women rented plots in their own right, and more may have taken on plots when husbands or fathers fell ill, or when they became widows. In Warwickshire, for example, widows appear on nearly every list of rural allotments in the early nineteenth century. Yet on the

ALLOTMENTS.

IT COST ME MONEY, WEEKS OF TOIL,
IN RAIN, AND WIND, AND SUN,
AND NOW I'VE DUG THE TATIES UP,
I'VE ONLY GROWN JUST ONE.

whole, rural allotments were the men's place, keeping them out of the house and, to the joy of the local clergy, out of the ale house. A government report of 1867 had declared that working on the land would "almost unsex a woman" and create social mischief by "unfitting or indisposing her for a woman's proper duties at home", and so it is not surprising that the women on the lists of plot tenants are mainly widows.

Some urban allotment sites were originally established as "guinea gardens" (more correctly but less alliteratively called "detached urban gardens"). These were generally allotment-sized plots (typically 10 or 20 poles, 10 poles being 300 square yards/250 square metres), rented on a commercial basis by land-holders and developers to the burgeoning middle classes of shopkeepers and tradesmen. Denied a garden attached to their house by dint of living over

ABOVE LEFT: As allotments became fashionable in the immediate pre- and post-war periods, a series of comic postcards was issued on allotment life.

OUT FOR VICTORY.

THE ALLOTMENT HOLDER.
Too old to fight, but doing his bit to beat the U boats.

the shop and often having only a small yard or a courtyard used for business, these middle-class families paid considerably more than the average allotment holder for the delights of having a plot. England may have been a nation of shopkeepers, but its shopkeepers also gardened. Unlike regular allotments, the plots were usually hedged round, or even fenced; they could be used for flowers and lawns and fruit trees, as well as vegetables, and many even boasted small brick summerhouses or glasshouses. At Warwick, the Hill Close guinea gardens had a view across the valley to the south towards the Warwick racecourse;

ALLOTMENT FEVER

WYMONDHAM
PARISH COUNCIL.

CULTIVATION OF COTTAGE GARDENS AND ALLOTMENTS.

Owners or Occupiers of Cottage Gardens or Allotments in the above Parish, who are unable to cultivate the same, are invited to apply to the Parish Council for advice and help, at the same time giving the reason for non-cultivation.

Persons requiring Plots of land for cultivation should also apply to the above Council.

Applications made under this notice should be sent to the Clerk to the Council at his office in Vicar Street, Wymondham, on or before Monday the 5th March next.

JOHN B. POMEROY,
WYMONDHAM,   **Clerk to the Council.**
21st February, 1917.

H. G. STONE, PRINTER, WYMONDHAM.

LEFT: In response to the Kaiser's threat to starve Britain into submission, an enquiry was issued into the number of vacant plots on allotment sites. This poster was issued within days of the Kaiser's speech.

LARK RISE PLOTS

"The women never worked in the vegetable gardens or on the allotments, even when they had their children off [their] hand and had plenty of spare time, for there was a strict division of labour, and that was 'men's work'. Victorian ideas, too, had penetrated to some extent and any work outside the home was considered unwomanly. But even that code permitted a woman to cultivate a flower garden …"

Flora Thompson, looking back on her nineteenth-century rural childhood in Lark Rise to Candleford *(1939)*

---

in Cambridge (a county also rich in allotment sites) "guinea gardens" were placed around the more pastoral suburbs, including the Newnham and Girton areas. Wherever trade was burgeoning, there also were detached gardens: Birmingham, Coventry, Nottingham and Sheffield all boasted their little pieces of Eden. As they were more in the nature of a flower garden, women were more likely to take an active role in these sites.

With the outbreak of the First World War in 1914, the provision of allotments was no longer a matter for political protest, and became instead a national duty. In February 1917, Kaiser Wilhelm famously threatened that, with the aid of the U Boats, Germany would "... frighten the British flag off the face of the waters and starve the British people until they, who have refused

peace, will kneel and plead for it". Suddenly the race was on to turn land into allotments and grow as much food as possible. Parks and playing fields, commons and "wastes" were all ploughed up and turned over to the spade and the hoe. Epping Forest was opened to cultivators for the first time, the gardens opposite Buckingham Palace grew veg instead of geraniums, and Prime Minister Lloyd George turned his own garden over to potatoes. Enquiries were instigated into plots that lay uncultivated or unlet. The number of allotments soared from about 450,000 to over 1.5 million in 1918 – with railway allotments alone rising from 27,680 to 93,471. Allotments became not only patriotic but also fashionable. "Allotments", declared one contemporary writer, "have now become woven into the texture of our national life."

At the end of the First World War there was heartbreak for many an allotment holder as plots on requisitioned land had to be given back. At first, demand for allotments remained high, with over 7,000 applicants each week in 1919, as returning serviceman put pressure on household budgets, but a general air of discouragement set in and the numbers of plots gradually dropped until they amounted to only slightly more than before the war. There was of course always a core of proud allotment holders, and for many the food produced on the allotment must have seen them through the bad years of depression during the 1930s.

In the autumn of 1939, allotments again became the focus of the nation's effort with the outbreak of the Second World War. Determined not to be caught on the hop again, the government had already planned its emergency wartime measures and it was not long before the Allotment Army marched out to the potato trenches in an effort to win the Food War. At least they

ABOVE: From the early 1900s onwards, amateur magazines often included "allotments" in their headlines — realizing that many of their readers did most of their gardening down on the plot.

BELOW: A whole village appears to have turned out to do its bit in this First World War era photograph.

OPPOSITE: It was all hands to the hoe from 1917 onwards, including for the first time women and children on the allotment — previously a male stronghold.

ALLOTMENT FEVER

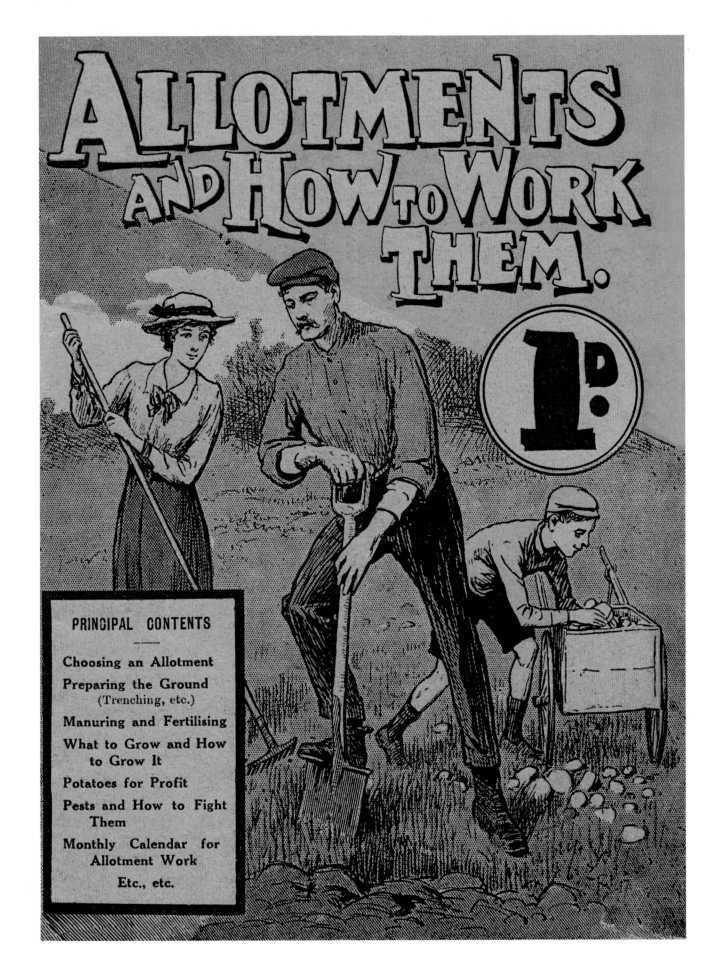

ALLOTMENTS AND HOW TO WORK THEM.

1^D

PRINCIPAL CONTENTS

Choosing an Allotment

Preparing the Ground
(Trenching, etc.)

Manuring and Fertilising

What to Grow and How
to Grow It

Potatoes for Profit

Pests and How to Fight
Them

Monthly Calendar for
Allotment Work

Etc., etc.

would have done, but the war broke out at what, for gardeners, was a rather inconvenient time of year. For old hands, late autumn marks the start of the new year, with plots to be dug over in time to let the frost break down the clods to fine tilth, and winter greens (planted many months ago) firming up nicely. Cottager's kale, also known as "hungry gap kale", stands firm over winter to provide through the empty months of early spring. But for the half million new allotment holders, initial confusion over how to get an allotment – with the local councils tripping over the National Allotments and Gardens Society to organize provision – meant that most did not move on to the land until November and were then faced with a very different prospect to the established allotmenter who had a well-dug plot to contemplate. Wartime allotments were created either on suburban fringes, previously earmarked for building and often carved from large agricultural strips, or on inner-city parks and pleasure gardens. Both had their disadvantages, although the building plots had the advantage of not needing to be stripped of turf – a necessary activity that had one Cambridge man in the local courts when he carefully wheeled away the turf rather than building a turf stack with it to use later as soil conditioner! He was fined five shillings for his ignorance.

Those who managed to acquire an allotment in that first winter soon regretted it. The winter and spring of 1939–40 were among the worst on record, with the

ALLOTMENT RULES AND REGULATIONS

- Every Occupier will be expected to attend some Place of Public Worship at least Once Every Sunday, and should he neglect to do so without sufficient cause, will be deprived of his Land;
- Any Occupier guilty of Dishonesty, or Theft, will be deprived of his Land;
- Any Member getting vegetables in the Garden Fields after Nine O'Clock on a Sunday Morning ... Will be Fined Sixpence;
- Any Member laying Dung on the Gravel Roads will be fined One Shilling for the First Offence and for the second offence he will be expelled from the Club;
- The Land Shall be cultivated by the Spade only;
- All tenants shall maintain a character for morality and sobriety and shall not frequent a public-house on the Sabbath-Day;
- All the tenants are earnestly requested to attend regularly at the House of God during the times of Divine Service, with their families;
- No Allotment or Part-of shall be Under-let;
- At Least X Load of Manure shall be laid on Each Allotment Every year.

Taken from the lists of the Lyddington Gardens (near Swindon), the Rothamsted Allotment Club (where there were "Members" rather than "Tenants") and the Church Field Allotments, Sharnbrook.

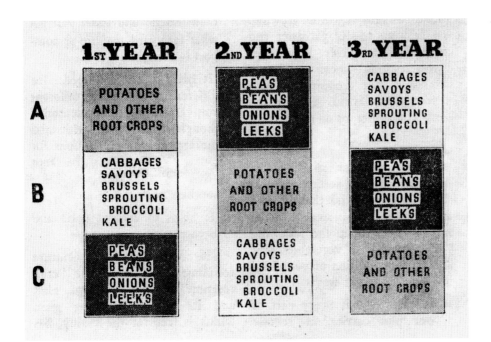

1ST YEAR	2ND YEAR	3RD YEAR
A POTATOES AND OTHER ROOT CROPS	PEAS BEANS ONIONS LEEKS	CABBAGES SAVOYS BRUSSELS SPROUTING BROCCOLI KALE
B CABBAGES SAVOYS BRUSSELS SPROUTING BROCCOLI KALE	POTATOES AND OTHER ROOT CROPS	PEAS BEANS ONIONS LEEKS
C PEAS BEANS ONIONS LEEKS	CABBAGES SAVOYS BRUSSELS SPROUTING BROCCOLI KALE	POTATOES AND OTHER ROOT CROPS

OPPOSITE: Proudly displaying his onions, this plot holder appears to be one of the many white-collar workers who held urban allotments. Urban sites were often much larger than rural, to cater for the larger populations of the towns.

LEFT: This basic three-year rotational plan for a 10-pole plot was issued by the Ministry of Agriculture towards the end of the war — stressing the need for continued effort through what were to become known as the austerity years. At the outbreak of war in 1939, crop rotation had been promoted cautiously as no one wanted to admit the war might last that long!

coldest winter for 45 years and the coldest February since records began. Winter cabbages froze to their very hearts and even the toughest winter spinach wilted in the icy onslaught. The government's cheerful advice to "Plan for Winter as Well as Summer" (the theme of their first "Dig for Victory" leaflet) seemed hollow as temperatures plummeted. To add to the troubles of the plot holder, tools were in short supply and wheelbarrows even shorter – with one gardening periodical recommending one wheelbarrow between five plots. In towns that achieved the government's target of one allotment for every five households, the numbers of wheelbarrows must have been sufficient to cause a small traffic jam! Some towns achieved considerably more than this target – especially after the announcement of a further half a million plots in October 1940. By summer 1940, the traditional "allotment" counties of Yorkshire and Lancashire already had 62,000 and 34,000 allotments respectively. In February 1941, the Royal Borough of Windsor had over 1,300 allotments; Heston and Isleworth (Middlesex) had 3,660 allotments (one for every seven households); Gravesend had 1,150 allotments at the same date; and Cardiff over 3,000 war-time allotments (in addition to normal peace-time allotments). By the spring of 1945, Thetford in Norfolk had one allotment for every two households, and Sittingbourne (Kent) was not far behind with 2,000 allotments between 5,000 houses.

By the end of the war, it was estimated that more than half of all working-class families were Digging for Victory, either on an allotment or in their own garden. As one gardening periodical put it, "During the war it is the duty of every able-bodied person who has the necessary time and land, to grow sufficient vegetables for his or her own family ... It is the duty of every parish council, urban council or county borough to provide land for allotments for all those who require land."

As novice plot holders diligently followed the advice of the numerous "Dig for Victory" leaflets (issued literally in the millions), they were encouraged by the presence of model allotments or demonstration plots in many public parks or high-profile sites – such as Kew Gardens. Here beleaguered park officials were instructed to follow government guidance dutifully to the letter to show what could be achieved on a 10-pole plot. The Ministry of Agriculture claimed that these plots would prove "of first class educational, propaganda and psychological value". In fact, they usually ended up the centre of attention for that most common of gardeners: the one whose crops are earlier, larger and generally better than the ones on show.

To encourage even more competition amongst plot holders, the government set up a scheme to award certificates of merit to those allotment holders whose plots "in the opinion of the judges, are best cultivated to produce a continuous supply of the most suitable vegetables throughout the year. Every allotment entered for the competition will be visited twice by the judges, who will give points for cultivation, rotation, planning, compost heap, control of weeds etc." Over 10,000 plot holders vied for the coveted certificates in one year alone, with 4,000 achieving the required standard. If you did not feel the need for a certificate, you could simply purchase a badge from the National Allotments Society for 3d and proclaim to all your commitment to Digging for Victory.

In 1944, it was announced that allotmenters and backyarders had between them produced 10 per cent of the nation's food during the war and numbers of allotment plots had risen to an all-time high, estimated at 1.5 to 2 million plots – although numbers were difficult to track as some councils calculated by acres rather than numbers. Alas, it was not to last. With the end of the war came an end to plots of requisitioned land and, as with the aftermath of the First World War, once again the plot holders found they had little or no protection from eviction. What the government propaganda promised with one announcement, it took away with the next. Despite the Minister of Agriculture's declaration to the assembled plot holders at the annual National Allotments and Gardens Society that "Today we are digging for our very lives, for food, for dollars and for self-respect", the closure of the war-time sites dealt a heavy blow, and was followed by the loss of over one-fifth of all public allotment sites in the decade that followed. The 1960s saw worse to come, with half of all private plots being closed as railways sold land and rationalized and reduced lines after the 1963 Beeching Report, whilst that other great landholder, the church, was forced to look for economies and ways to fund repairs. But it was not really the landholders who were ringing the death knell for allotments – it was society as a whole. The Sixties famously "swung" and if there was one thing that didn't

ABOVE: The Royal Horticultural Society and the EWMFS both encouraged allotment and cottage-garden holders to compete — something that would be continued by the government during the Second Word War.

ALLOTMENT FEVER

swing it was allotments. Two decades on from the height of the Dig for Victory campaign, for the younger generation allotments represented austerity, war and old men in flat caps. The take-up of allotments was at a low point, and in the words of the government's Thorpe Report, "one in five plots lay abandoned ... with weeds flourishing waist high" and fluttering plastic pennants scared birds from non-existent crops. Professor Thorpe (a landscape architect) found the taint of make-do-and-mend alive and well on the sites, with ramshackle huts made of old air-raid shelters. The heroic endeavours of the Allotment Army had sunk once more beneath the "stink of charity and economic motive". Thorpe was poised to revolutionize the humble allotment into a new "leisure garden" concept, replete with community sheds, cul-de-sacs and car parking. New name, new social class and lots of valuable land released for building. But the green revolution struck back as the "good life" gained ground and organics replaced swing. By 1974, demand for allotments exceeded supply for the first time in decades and local councils came under fire for their lack of enthusiasm and commitment to the world of the plot. Concerns about pesticides, GM foods, air miles and climate change followed, and soon there were queues outside the gates of sites with plots to let. Policies such as urban greening, community development, sustainable living and even "outdoor gyms" led to the Allotments Regeneration Initiative in 2003 and soon a new generation of allotment holders was born. Intent on Digging for Life rather than for Victory, the Allotment Army marches on.

OPPOSITE: Standing proudly to attention with their forks and potatoes, this group of working-class men (with one token woman!) epitomizes everything the Swinging Sixties hated about allotments. Fifty years on, over half of allotment plots are taken by women on some sites.

BELOW: The new green image of allotments incorporates plots in various stages of their life cycles, from weeds to crops and back again, and allotment art has made a resurgence with the wildlife.

8

Digging for Victory; Digging for Peace

PREVIOUS PAGE: Suburban back gardens were transformed during the war into Britain's "line of defence" against the enemy.

RIGHT: Stephen Cheveley, author of *A Garden Goes to War*, was the gardening correspondent of *The Times*. In his book he describes the very first days after the announcement of war, when he dug up his lawn for root vegetables and cleared the herbaceous borders for beans.

A GARDEN GOES TO WAR

BY STEPHEN CHEVELEY

On 3 September 1939, King George VI called on the nation to "stand calm, firm and united in this time of trial", as Britain declared war on Germany. Exactly one month later, on 3 October, the Minister of Agriculture first urged the nation to Dig for Victory. The Dig for Victory campaign was to become the most successful Home Front campaign of the war, and possibly the most memorable government slogan ever. It was the slogan that almost never was, as the government had settled on the rather less inspiring "Grow More Food", but the media leapt on the catchy alternative and soon the nation's gardens were transformed into Victory gardens: lawns were sacrificed for lettuces and bedding for brassicas. Everywhere was upheaval as amateurs and professionals alike converted their hobby into a patriotic duty, even going so far as to encourage hens and rabbits into the lovingly tended herbaceous borders. Plans to convert peace-time gardens into war-time producers filled every gardening periodical and even air-raid shelters were used to grow radishes and marrows. For five years gardening hints appeared in newspapers, magazines and even on leaflets posted through the door. The Dig for Victory slogan was used for advertising products as diverse as whisky and furniture polish. By 1945 at least half of all working-class households were busy growing their own – or, as the government preferred to see it, growing for the nation. But the war changed the nation's gardens in more ways than simply by replacing carnations with cabbages. The devastation of flower nurseries and glasshousing, shortages of equipment, the requisitioning of country-house parks and gardens and the tearing down of park railings were all to have a lasting effect.

In 1938, England imported over 55 million tons of fresh vegetables, including almost two million pounds' worth of onions and four-and-a-half million pounds' worth of tomatoes (at 1938 prices). Over 90 per cent of onions were imported from France, Spain and Egypt, while tomatoes came from Holland. Even apples, once the famed produce of the "orchard of England", were imported in their millions. With the ports blockaded and ships needed for military service, the importation of fresh and canned foods was at best curtailed and after the German occupation of much of Europe in 1940, many imports were eventually cut off all together. Britain's gardens were to be her "line of defence" and cropping plans her secret weapon. Owing to the massive inter-war expansion of the suburbs, millions more households had become divorced from the farmyard and countryside, and would be dependent on what they could grow in their own gardens and allotments. For many, vegetable gardening was a new experience, even if they had pottered in the flower borders of their Tudorbethan semis. The Dig for Victory campaign aimed to provide these novices with advice, encouragement and outright cajolery – with the occasional threat thrown in.

On 16 September 1939, *Garden Work for Amateurs* enthused its readers for the task ahead:

> *In the great conflict ahead of us, we who stay at home can play just as important a part as those in the firing line … We urge all our readers to make every effort to enlarge their cultivations of vegetable and fruit crops.*

Whether it was the encouragement of *Garden Work* or the government, or a very sensible fear of being left short of food, within the first weeks of war breaking out, lawns all over the country were being sacrificed and chrysanthemums and dahlias, gay in their autumn colours, were heading for the compost heap. The garden writer Stephen Cheveley recorded that:

Cecil Henry Middleton (1886–1945) was the voice of wartime gardening. Every Sunday afternoon at 2.15 pm millions of gardeners, and non-gardeners, settled round the family wireless to listen to his gently soporific voice. His style was chatty, friendly and personal. He shared his listeners' triumphs and their failures and, despite having to toe the government line, he also sympathized with the difficulties they faced over seed and fertilizer shortages and lack of time. Mr Middleton himself was particularly short of time, being sent all over the country to appear on Dig for Victory gardeners' question panels, as well as writing books and making short film bulletins for the cinemas; he even appeared on television briefly, before it was turned off for the duration of the war. In one broadcast, he told of returning to his home and garden in Surbiton to find it devastated by birds and weeds after a long absence. Mr Middleton came from a gardening family – his father was a head gardener – but he never assumed any knowledge amongst his listeners. In the words of the writer and critic Wilfrid Rooke Ley, "He will assume that your soil is poor, and your pocket poor. All he asks is that your hopes are high and your Saturday afternoons at his service … He stands for common sense and has the gift of consolation." Mr Middleton died on 18 September 1945, having brought the nation's novice gardeners successfully through the Dig for Victory campaign.

ABOVE: Mr Middleton became a household name during the war, and appeared in books, magazines, adertisements, cartoon strips and even short information films.

On a Saturday afternoon, early in September, my young son and I cleared the border. We cut off all flowers worth taking into the house; whole plants of chrysanthemums were executed, and they made a glorious bunch in a huge bowl in the hall. After the first unhappy twinges of regret we became keen on the job, and once the flowers were out of the way it didn't seem nearly so bad.

Other gardeners were more cautious and tried – perhaps less successfully – to insert tomatoes and runner beans in amongst the roses. In larger gardens, the tennis court was often chosen as the sacrifice, being a large open space that would perhaps get little use in the years to follow. Petrol rationing meant that motor-mowers were soon a thing of the past, so any lawns left in place soon took on a shaggy look. *The Gardeners' Chronicle* suggested sheep as an alternative for larger lawns. The one area that even the most ardent digger for victory left untouched was the rock garden. A popular feature in the 1930s, when most small suburban gardens boasted a pile of rocks, or at least clinker and concrete, this was of little use for root vegetables or even brassicas, and continued to be planted with alpines and pinks through the war.

In the first months of the war, the Ministry of Agriculture issued three "Growmore" bulletins advising gardeners what to plant, how to plant it and how to protect it from various pests and diseases. These early leaflets were quite long and detailed, and cost the patriotic gardener 3d each. They were not the success the government was hoping for. Bowing to popular pressure, the government quietly ditched "Grow More" in favour of "Dig for Victory", at the same time adopting the "foot and spade" symbol that was to become the iconic symbol of the campaign. Mr Mckie of Acton, London, was the owner of the famous (left) foot which appeared, disconcertingly disembodied, over the spade. Digging with the left foot was the traditional technique for those who were right-handed, believed to result in a less twisted action whilst digging.

With the re-launch of the Dig for Victory campaign in the early autumn of 1940 came a renewed push to get the nation gardening. The loss of food supplies, following the German invasion of much of mainland Europe that summer, brought home the realization that the United Kingdom would have to provide for herself. As the Battle of Britain raged overhead during the summer and autumn of 1940, gardeners dug in below. The question of what and how much to grow was tackled by the first Dig for Victory leaflet, which provided a cropping plan for an "average" garden or allotment, sufficient to keep three adults and two children in fresh food for eight months of the year (the other four months presumably being covered by stored foods). Potatoes, parsnips, cabbages, carrots, spinach (winter and summer), beetroot, leeks, runner beans (then known as "scarlet beans"), broad beans and peas were the basics – providing carbohydrates, vitamins and proteins. These were supplemented with lettuce, tomatoes, radishes and outdoor cucumber in the summer. Onions were grown to give flavour

BELOW: Although traditional village shows, with their giant onions and flower arrangements, were discouraged during the war, they were replaced with Dig for Victory shows and Red Cross shows which emphasized efficient growing of foodstuffs.

BOTTOM: An immaculate lawn goes on "war duty". Note the digger is using his left foot.

BON MARCHE (Gloucester) LTD.
DIG FOR VICTORY CAMPAIGN
Class No. 24.
FIRST PRIZE
Name Miss Zoote.
Exhibit TOMATOES.

THIS PLAN WILL GIVE YOU YOUR OWN VEGETABLES ALL THE YEAR ROUND

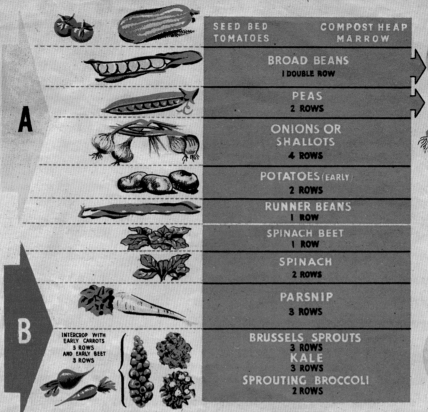

SEED BED TOMATOES — **COMPOST HEAP MARROW**

A

B

INTERCROP WITH
EARLY CARROTS
3 ROWS
AND EARLY BEET
3 ROWS

BROAD BEANS
I DOUBLE ROW

PEAS
2 ROWS

ONIONS OR SHALLOTS
4 ROWS

POTATOES (EARLY)
2 ROWS

RUNNER BEANS
I ROW

SPINACH BEET
I ROW

SPINACH
2 ROWS

PARSNIP
3 ROWS

BRUSSELS SPROUTS
3 ROWS
KALE
3 ROWS
SPROUTING BROCCOLI
2 ROWS

INTERCROP AND FOLLOW WITH SUMMER LETTUCE

FOLLOW WITH LEEKS 4 ROWS

Rotation Diagram

A B
B A

ALLOTMENT OR GARDEN

PLOT . . . . . 45' x 30'

APPROX. 5 SQ. RODS POLES OR PERCHES

TABLE OF PLANTING AND PERIOD OF USE
WINTER SUPPLIES PRINTED IN GREEN

CROP	TIME OF SOWING	DISTANCE APART		PERIOD OF USE
		Rows	Plants	
BEANS (Broad)	**Feb.-March**	1 double row	6 in. by 9 in.	July
BEANS (Runner)	**Mid-May**		9 in.	July-Oct.
BEET	April	15 in.	6 in. (thin)	July-April
BROCCOLI (Sprouting) ..	Mid-May / Plant Mid-July	2 ft.	2 ft.	April-May
BRUSSELS SPROUTS ..	March / Plant May-June	2½ ft.	2½ ft.	Nov.-Mar.
CARROTS (Early) ..	**April**	1 ft.	6 in. (thin)	June-Sept.
KALE	May / Plant Mid.-July	2 ft.	2 ft.	Jan.-April
LEEKS	March / Plant July	1 ft.	6 in. / 9 in.	Mar.-May
LETTUCE ...	**March and every 14 days**	**Between other crops**	9 in.	May-Oct.
MARROW	**May**		3-4 ft.	July-Feb.
ONIONS	Mid.-Feb.	1 ft.	6 in. (thin)	July-June
PARSNIPS	Mid.-Feb.-Mid.-March	15 in.	6 in. (thin)	Nov.-Mar.
PEAS	**March and April**	2½ ft.	3 in.	June-July
POTATOES (Early) ..	**March**	2 ft.	1 ft.	July-Aug.
SHALLOTS	February	1 ft.	6 in.	Jan.-Dec.
SPINACH (Winter) ..	Sept.	1 ft.	6 in. (thin)	Spring
SPINACH BEET ..	April	8 in.	8 in. (groups)	July-Oct. and Jan.-June
TOMATOES	**Plant end May**		15 in.	Aug.-Oct.

Printed for H.M. Stationery Office by T. G. Porter (Printers) Ltd., Leeds. 51-3308

to increasingly meatless meals, and marrows proved ever popular because they grew so easily and could be used to bulk out nearly anything from jam to stew. Herbs, if grown at all, were usually restricted to parsley, mint and thyme – supplies of the latter having been imported from Germany before the war.

Some vegetables were regarded as either too difficult or time-consuming for the amateur or novice gardener. Cauliflowers were very temperamental, needing moist but not wet soil, cool days and frost-free nights. They also needed a range of fertilizers and supplements, as well as the tying over of the leaves to produce the clean white heads – not a vegetable for the hectic days of war, when gardening had to be combined with ARP (Air Raid Precautions) duty or work in a factory. Asparagus was regarded as a wasteful food, occupying much space for little return, and celery was also viewed by the government as consuming too much work for little return in nutrition, although there were protests from northern gardeners who claimed that "In many northern counties a tea-table is not considered complete without cheese and celery accompanying it". On the other hand, spinach, seakale and salsify (to name just a few) were apparently almost unheard-of north of Durham.

Gooseberries maintained their prime position as home-grown fruit, being packed with goodness – according to the adverts. At first, the government was shy of encouraging gardeners to plant fruit trees and bushes, reckoning that

OPPOSITE: The government's main worry was that people would only plant easy-to-grow salad stuffs, leaving the nation hungry over winter.

ABOVE LEFT: The first of many… This Growmore Bulletin, containing detailed information on all aspects of vegetable growing, was issued by the government in the first month of the war. Later these were to be replaced by the shorter, more accessible Dig for Victory leaflets.

ABOVE: Perhaps the most famous foot in the nation's history! The foot belonged to Mr Mckie of Acton, London, and was to be featured on all Dig for Victory posters, leaflets and advertisements for the next five years! It was reproduced millions of times in scales from ½ inch (1 centimetre) to 15 feet (4.5 metres)!

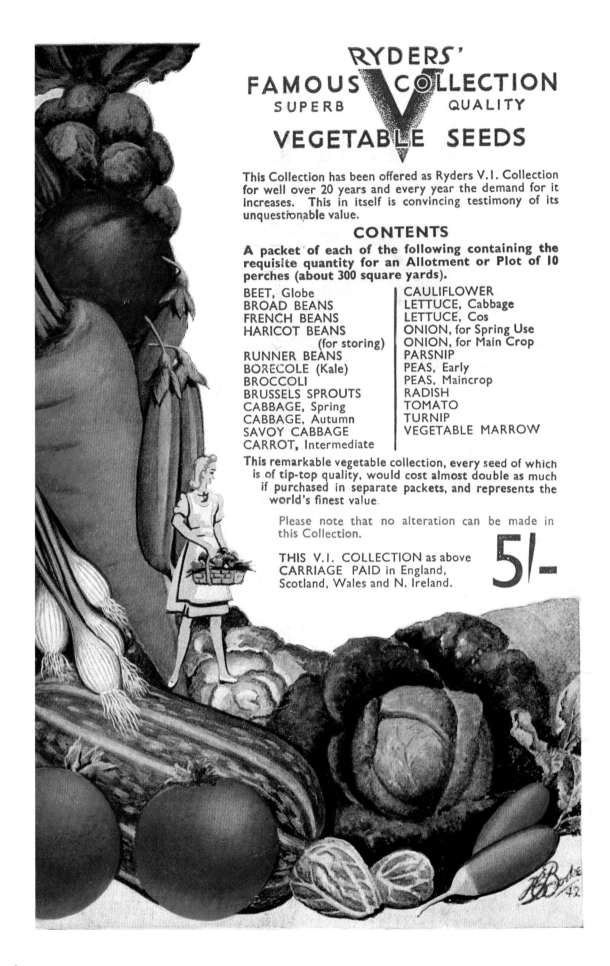

RYDERS'
FAMOUS COLLECTION
SUPERB QUALITY
VEGETABLE SEEDS

This Collection has been offered as Ryders V.I. Collection for well over 20 years and every year the demand for it increases. This in itself is convincing testimony of its unquestionable value.

CONTENTS

A packet of each of the following containing the requisite quantity for an Allotment or Plot of 10 perches (about 300 square yards).

BEET, Globe
BROAD BEANS
FRENCH BEANS
HARICOT BEANS
      (for storing)
RUNNER BEANS
BORECOLE (Kale)
BROCCOLI
BRUSSELS SPROUTS
CABBAGE, Spring
CABBAGE, Autumn
SAVOY CABBAGE
CARROT, Intermediate

CAULIFLOWER
LETTUCE, Cabbage
LETTUCE, Cos
ONION, for Spring Use
ONION, for Main Crop
PARSNIP
PEAS, Early
PEAS, Maincrop
RADISH
TOMATO
TURNIP
VEGETABLE MARROW

This remarkable vegetable collection, every seed of which is of tip-top quality, would cost almost double as much if purchased in separate packets, and represents the world's finest value.

Please note that no alteration can be made in this Collection.

THIS V.I. COLLECTION as above
CARRIAGE PAID in England,
Scotland, Wales and N. Ireland.

5/-

DIGGING FOR VICTORY; DIGGING FOR PEACE

the war would be over by the time they produced fruit, and in some places old orchards were even grubbed up to be put under the plough for potatoes. But Dig for Victory leaflet No. 25 (issued late in the campaign) gave instructions on how to renovate old fruit trees. Strawberries, that most traditional taste of English summers, were also quietly ignored by the official Dig for Victory campaign as, like asparagus, they took up a lot of ground year round for just one short season of cropping. Market gardeners could be prosecuted for harbouring too many strawberry plants, and acres of productive plants in Essex and Kent had to be uprooted to make way for more essential crops at the outbreak of war. Those who obeyed government instructions and then found themselves short of home-grown fruit were told to use swede, parsnip and carrots as substitutes and many a child brought up during the war found difficulty adapting to real bananas after years of the parsnip substitute.

The 1940s diet was not an adventurous one, and courgettes and aubergines were almost unheard-of. Kohl Rabi, ideal for novice gardeners and in plentiful supply as seed over the war years, was treated suspiciously by housewives, as were Jerusalem artichokes. Garlic, if eaten at all, was consumed despite its aftertaste and widely regarded as the worst feature of Mediterranean cookery! Sweetcorn, which arrived in gift parcels of seeds sent over from America, was usually grown only to feed the hens – a fact which would have mortified those sending the parcels, had they known. Less likely to be fed to hens were tobacco plants. Supplies of cigarettes and tobacco were sporadic during the war and many gardeners tried to grow their own, drying it in glasshouses or even in the oven. Although it was not illegal to grow tobacco, it was illegal to smoke your own, as there was a tax on tobacco for

OPPOSITE: Many seed companies issued special Victory Packs of seeds containing everything listed in the government's Dig for Victory leaflet No. 1. The cost of these varied from a basic mixed pack of non-specified varieties, for as little as 3s, to an expanded pack for a larger family with named varieties, for as much as 12s 6d. This advertisement for Ryders' V collection shows a woman, which was unusual even during wartime.

ABOVE LEFT: During the war local horticultural and flower shows continued under the guise of "victory shows", many raising funds for the Red Cross. Competitors were supposed to concentrate on production of a range of "official" victory vegetables rather than the more time-consuming and wasteful "largest onion in show" etc that had been traditionally popular. However, few could resist the challenge of growing the largest marrow or pumpkin!

ABOVE: Before the Second World War lots of apples and pears were imported from mainland Europe and our own orchards had in many cases fallen into disrepair. In 1942, the government started a campaign to bring these neglected orchards and old trees and bush fruits in private gardens back into production.

Second Impression

The
Vegetable Garden displayed

1/3
Postage 3ᵈ

Royal Horticultural Society, London

ABOVE: Despite the government issue of Dig for Victory leaflets on every subject imaginable, many gardeners found further guidance in the RHS's *The Vegetable Garden Displayed*. Illustrating each stage of each task, it revolutionized gardening instruction. After the war, it was translated into German and copies were sent to help the defeated nations feed themselves.

BELOW: Death and destruction were high on the list of tasks for the wartime gardener.

OPPOSITE: Identifying pests was made easier with the advice issued by gardening periodicals. Many novice gardeners mistook centipedes and millipedes, and one Victory gardener wrote in to say she had killed all the red-and-black "insects" on her plants, only to be told she had massacred all the aphid-eating ladybirds.

consumption, and so the pungent home-made smokes were best confined to puffing in the garden shed.

In the early Dig for Victory leaflets, the government gave specific recommendations for varieties which would best suit the home gardener. These included many of the tried and tested varieties with names evocative of Victorian nurserymen, large country-house gardens and distinguished Edwardian gardeners. Onions included Rousham Park Hero, Banbury Danvers Yellow and James's Long Keeping. For those brave enough (or foolhardy enough) to attempt to grow cauliflowers, they could choose from Veitch's Autumn Giant or All the Year Round. Peas and kale revealed their humble origins with varieties such as Rentpayer (peas) and Cottager Kale. Other varieties appear to have been chosen for their military resonance: Onward and Advance Guard were both early varieties of pea. Perhaps most memorable was the potato Home Guard developed in 1942 as a wart-resistant all-round heavy cropper, although often described as tasteless by the eventual consumer.

The issue of a new leaflet recommending specific varieties often resulted in rush of demand which outstripped the limited supply, and each re-issue saw different varieties included or the despairing note that supplies of the next season's seeds were not yet secure. An added complication was the shortage of tall poles or sticks for the support of taller varieties of peas, tomatoes and runner beans, such that by 1942 dwarf varieties were being recommended.

For those battling on the Garden Front, the enemy came in the form of pests and diseases. Pests such as rats, rabbits, snails, caterpillars and weevil were blamed for losses of vital foodstuffs and hotly pursued with everything from guns to nicotine spray. Diseases were often more of a mystery to the novice gardener, and traditional (if graphic) names such as "Finger and Toe Disease" (club root), wart disease or silvery leaf blight gave the feel of a gothic novel to the vegetable plot. The Ministry of Agriculture placed advertisements to encourage people in the battle against pests. An anti-rat campaign declared that 30 million pounds of food was destroyed by rats every year. Underneath a drawing of a rat with a Hitler moustache, the adverts declared "The fight is on!" against these ravenous pests. Butterflies, it was claimed, were flocking in from the Continent with the specific aim of stripping the nation's food supply. In 1943, *The Gardeners' Chronicle* estimated that 15,000,000 cabbage white butterflies had invaded England from the enemy-occupied mainland, causing despair amongst gardeners and farmers alike.

VEGETABLE PEST CONTROL

PEST OR DISEASE	DAMAGE DONE	REMEDY
ASPARAGUS : Beetle............	Defoliation	Dust with DDT powder.
BEAN : Aphis (Black Fly).......	Distorts and weakens	Dust with derris or nicotine. Spray with BHC.
Weevil	Notching of leaves........	Dust or spray with DDT, BHC, lindane, derris or dieldrin.
Slugs.....................	Growths eaten. Attack many kinds of vegetables, including Potatoes	Use metaldehyde bait or water with Slugit.
BRASSICAS (BRUSSELS SPROUTS, CABBAGE, BROCCOLI, etc.) :		
Aphis (Mealy)...............	Feeds in colonies on under-sides of leaves.	Apply BHC (benzene hexachloride) or lindane spray forcefully, or dust with derris.
Caterpillars	Leaves eaten	Apply DDT, BHC, lindane or derris dusts or sprays.
Cutworms..................	Stems eaten at soil level ..	Hoe in BHC or aldrin dusts.
Flea Beetle.................	Leaves punctured, especially in seedling stage.	Apply BHC, aldrin or lindane dusts 4-5 days after sowing and repeat in 10 days.
Root Fly	Roots eaten, plants wilt...	Dust gamma-BHC, aldrin or lindane, or water with dieldrin, within 4 days of planting seedlings.
Turnip Gall Weevil	Galls on base of stem	As for Root Fly.
Club Root Disease...........	Roots distorted, plants wilt.	Lime soil well. Dust planting holes and roots with 4% calomel dust.
CARROT: Fly	Maggots bore into roots...	Dust along rows with gamma-BHC, aldrin, or lindane.
Wireworm..................	Roots eaten	Hoe in, or dust seed drills, with aldrin, gamma-BHC or lindane dusts.
CELERY: Leaf Miner...........	Tunnels in leaves........	Spray at intervals with DDT, nicotine or dieldrin.
Leaf Spot Disease...........	Leaves blotched & withered	Spray at fortnightly intervals with Bordeaux Mixture.
Leaf Spot Disease...........	Leaves discoloured	Spray with Bordeaux Mixture.
CUCUMBER: Aphis.............	Leaves distorted	Spray with derris.
Mildew	Leaves powdered white....	Spray with thiram fungicide.
Red Spider	Leaves bleached and growth stunted.	Spray with derris.
LEEK: White Tip..............	Leaves wither............	Spray with Bordeaux Mixture.
White Rot Disease	As for Onions	As for Onions.
LETTUCE: Aphis	Leaves distorted	Spray with derris.
Cutworms	Stem eaten at soil level....	Hoe in gamma-BHC or aldrin dust.
Leatherjackets	Roots eaten..............	Hoe in gamma-BHC or aldrin dust.
MINT: Rust Disease	Growths become distorted and die down early.	Cover bed with straw and burn in early autumn. Make new bed from shoot cuttings.
ONION: Onion Fly	Bulbs eaten by maggots....	Apply gamma-BHC or aldrin dust at loop stage and in early July.
White Rot Disease	Roots rot and seedlings wither and collapse.	Dust drills with 4% calomel powder before sowing.
PARSNIP: Carrot Fly	Maggot bore into roots....	As for Carrot.

KILL THAT RAT!

These ravenous pests destroy our precious food. They spread disease. The damage they do costs the nation thirty million pounds a year.

For years we have put up with them; now let's make an end of them. If there are rats on your ground, use baits and traps till the last one's dead—that's the only good rat there is.

Don't let one escape—for they breed at an incredible rate.

From today, then, the fight is on!

Your County War Agricultural Executive Committee is eager to help you. Ask them for a copy of the special Leaflet on Rat Destruction and Prevention.

ABOVE: Pests and diseases were identified as enemy agents, replete with Nazi flags or Hitler moustaches.

RIGHT: A concerned Ministry of Agriculture made pests and diseases the focus of their second Growmore Bulletin.

OPPOSITE: An incredible array of chemicals were available over the counter to deal with pests and diseases. Many have subsequently been banned.

PESTS & DISEASES IN THE VEGETABLE GARDEN

"GROWMORE" BULLETIN No. 2 OF THE MINISTRY OF AGRICULTURE AND FISHERIES PUBLISHED BY HIS MAJESTY'S STATIONERY OFFICE

Slugs were also a serious threat in the wet summers, especially with so many new vegetable plots placed close to grass. The traditional treatment was metaldehyde soaked into bran but, as war shortages bit, bran was in short supply and giving it to slugs was illegal. Other common substitutes, such as bread or potato, were also being used to feed pigs and hens (or humans) and were regarded as running the risk of being eaten by children. Hand-killing was an effective if time-consuming substitute – but not for the squeamish.

One of the more challenging aspects of gardening in wartime was the question of where in the garden to put the Anderson shelter. These shelters had been issued to householders since the spring of 1939, well before the actual declaration of war. In his popular book *Practical Gardening and Food Production in Pictures* (first issued in 1940 and running to numerous editions through the 1940s and '50s), Richard Suddell recommended that "the Anderson pattern air raid shelter is situated in an inconspicuous spot near the greenhouse" at the end of the garden. The access steps down to the buried shelter are shown, on Suddell's plan of "A Garden Adapted to Wartime Needs", as located in a bed of broccoli and kale, and one can only hope that they withstood the trampling! In August 1940, *Garden Work* ran an illustrated article on "Turning Your Dugout to Account" which celebrated the unexpected gardening opportunities presented by the ugly shelters. It admitted that, on the face of it, "A conspicuous object of this sort in what may be a small garden can be an eyesore (and undesirably conspicuous from the air, incidentally)," but went on to suggest that the shelter could be planted with vegetables, flowers or lawn. Marrows were the most popular option, being shallow-rooted, sprawling and appreciating the warmth provided by the shelter's roof slope. Spring bulbs were an alternative, although they did hint at longevity for this wartime feature and so annuals seemed somehow more patriotic, with their hints of an early conclusion to hostilities. Growing food on the shelter roofs offered the added triumph of turning "difficulties into account", in the words of the article, and there was even a suggestion that the amount of food grown on the shelters might outweigh in worth the inconveniences of bombing (this was before the the Blitz).

A later edition of *Garden Work* – obviously a periodical with an imaginative staff – extolled the virtues of planting climbers and bedding around the entrances of ARP posts. Suitable plants for such a site were listed under the heading "ARP Goes Gay". Other unlikely wartime gardening suggestions included converting shallow garden ponds into watercress beds and growing mushrooms in understairs cupboards. The satirical magazine *Punch* also ran a series of Home Front bulletins from the pen of "Lady Addle" (the literary invention of Mary Dunn), who recounted her gardening successes and failures, mainly the latter. These included growing mustard and cress on the garden statuary, planting tomatoes along the shady willow walk, and harvesting woolly aphids from the fruit trees.

The humorous "dispatches" of Lady Addle on the Home Front played on the very real tensions between the social classes during wartime and these were as apparent in gardening as in any other aspect of life. Whilst one in every two working-class households were said to be knuckling down to Digging for Victory, *The Gardeners' Chronicle*, a periodical aimed at professional gardeners and their employers, still dwelt on the difficulties of heating the orchid houses during coal rationing. *My Garden* (subtitled An Intimate Magazine for Garden Lovers) featured articles on snowdrops and dahlias and decried the loss of staff and the necessity to cut corners.

ABOVE: Few Anderson shelters were complete with welcoming garden gnomes!

OPPOSITE LEFT: Onion beds in a country-house rose garden. The central rose trellis has been left in, with roses still in flower. Perhaps a sacrifice too far?

OPPOSITE RIGHT: At Raynes Park, the home of Carters' Seed Company, the normally flower-filled beds were replaced with productive patterns of vegetables! The sundial gives away the original layout.

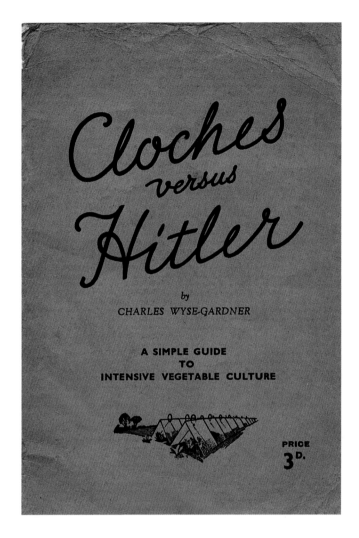

TURNING YOUR DUGOUT INTO ACCOUNT?

"Apart from food production, a dugout can be converted into the attractive rockery that nearly every gardener hankers after, but for lack of space is often deterred from undertaking. We have noticed several such war-time ornamental additions to gardens while travelling about the country."

Garden Work, 10 August 1940

Larger country houses were often badly hit by the war, with billeted troops, hospitals and schools causing irreparable damage to house and garden. Nissen huts sprung up everywhere, usually with concrete footings, and encampments sprawled across walled gardens and flower beds. A correspondent to *The Gardeners' Chronicle* remarked wistfully, "When one sees numbers of tents pitched and occupied by our troops, stretching almost throughout the whole length of some of our cherished herbaceous borders, one wishes that a larger number of our fighting men were plant lovers." Although some damage, such as shooting of statues or smashing of glasshouses, was deliberate, or at least the result of "high spirits", much was the outcome of essential wartime manoeuvres. Tanks practised amongst the ancient oaks and airfields sprung up on pasture accustomed to centuries of grazing deer herds.

Walled productive gardens, in many country houses only just recovered from the devastation wrought by the First World War, were once again thrown into disarray as vines and hot-house exotics were ousted to make way for tomatoes and lettuces. County War Agricultural Executive Committees (known as War Ags) ensured that those gardens which had enrolled in the government schemes

Clay's Fertilizer and first class seeds— a perfect combination for success in the Grow More Food campaign. For more than 70 years an ever increasing army of gardeners have used and accepted Clay's as the most reliable, economical and inexpensive plant food on the market. Little wonder then in the past year it leapt into instant popularity with the vast number of new recruits eager to grow more food. Put your faith in Clay's for 1941 and be sure of really heavy crops. Just remember to purchase a tin or bag with your seeds.

Tins 6d., 10d. & 1/6

Branded and Sealed Bags

7 lbs.	14 lbs.	28 lbs.	56 lbs.	112 lbs.
3/6	6/-	10/-	18/-	32/-

ONION PARSNIP TURNIP CABBAGE CARROT

FROM PACKET

TO PERFECTION

with **CLAY'S FERTILIZER**

Just the Feed Vegetables need

for food production grew only those fruit and vegetables approved by the Ministry of Agriculture. Gardens that joined the schemes were allowed to keep some of their garden staff, in contrast to private gardens where, regardless of what was grown, the gardeners were liable for conscription.

Some country-house gardens tried to combine decoration with productivity, planting tomatoes in the flower borders and carrots and beetroot – admired for their fancy foliage – in the parterres. Rose gardens grew runner beans and tennis courts were turned to camomile to help fill "the nation's medicine chest". The Women's Institutes led the way in collecting rosehips, digitalis (foxgloves), deadly nightshade and other traditional plants for use in medicines as stocks grew dangerously low, and Kew Gardens grew a camomile lawn to produce seeds for experimenting with easily disguised (and aromatic) airstrips around the country.

Slogans were everywhere during the war years, and the Garden Front was no exception. As well as Dig for Victory, other catchy mottos included "Better Planning, Better Crops", "The Need is Growing", "Beans as Bullets", "Dig to Keep Well Fed", "Grow for Winter as Well as Summer" and "An Hour with the Hoe Saves an Hour in the Queue". Building on the success of Dig for Victory, a whole host of slogans tried to keep up the impetus, from the straightforward "Dig On for Victory" to the rather pleasing "Dig for Plenty" and "Dig for Peace". "Dig for Dear Life" was a less popular suggestion. Advertisers also joined in, patriotically exhorting their customers to use "Cloches Versus

ABOVE: Fertilizers of all kinds were difficult to get hold of during the war. Farmers had priority for animal manures as well as chemical-based fertilizers. Hop-based fertilizer, commonly used before the war, became difficult to obtain after the hop fields of Kent were turned over to vegetable production. Experimentation by allotment holders resulted in a brisk trade in substitutes such as street sweepings, "shoddy" (from the textile industry) and even night soil. Clay's was one of the most popular fertilizers with home growers, although even they encountered supply problems.

Hitler", or protect their apple trees with "Mortegg Tar Wash – Holding the Maginot Line". Backyarders busy keeping hens on their allotment or suburban plot were informed that their chicks would "explode from their egg" if they used Lyddite hen feed, although hopefully the feed did not actually contain the high explosive lyddite.

Although everyone was encouraged to grow vegetables (rather than flowers) in wartime, many people still hankered after a little brightness in their lives. Flower seeds were available throughout the war, although in much less attractive packets and with some fluctuation in supply as the nurseries were put into wartime production. In order to try and discourage people from buying flower seed, nurseries were asked to charge for flower catalogues, whereas vegetable-seed catalogues were provided for free. Favourites were largely the same as during the inter-war years, with lupins, antirrhinums, phloxes and delphiniums giving height and colour to the border. Carnations and pinks provided a long season of trouble-free colour and the famous nursery of Allwoods sold a special selection of pinks which included the patriotically named "Spitfire" collection. Tulipland (based at Spalding, Lincolnshire) even released a special selection of tulips which could be planted to form a border or front garden in the national colours of red, white and blue. In 1945, the government gave way to increasing pressure, as flower seeds outsold vegetables for the first time since the war began, by allowing even allotment holders to include "a small fringe of colour" on the allotment, although this was not to take up more than ten per cent of the plot!

BELOW: Flower seeds, although available throughout the war, came in austerity packets. Novice gardeners were given no visual clue as to what the flowers would look like.

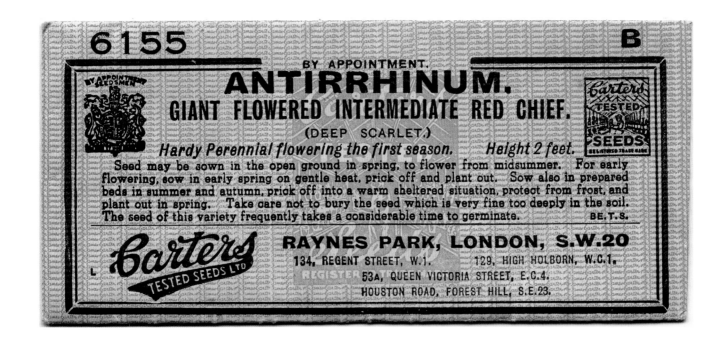

Nurseries and Seedsmen

THE
Compleat Gard'ner:
OR,
Directions for CULTIVATING
AND
Right ORDERING
OF
FRUIT-GARDENS,
AND
KITCHEN-GARDENS.

By Mounſieur De la Quintinye.

Now Compendiouſly Abridg'd, and made of more
Uſe, with very Conſiderable Improvements.

By George London, and Henry Wiſe.

The Second Edition, Corrected.

LONDON,
Printed for M. Gillyflower, and ſold by Andrew Bell at
the Croſs-Keys and Bible in Cornhil near Stocks-
Market, M DC XC IX.

To Noblemen, Gentlemen, and others.—An extensive and valuable
Nursery Stock, at Queen's Elms, Brompton.

MR. PHILLIPS will SELL by AUCTION,
on Monday, November 13, and five following days, punctu-
ally at One each day, at the Nursery Grounds of
Mr. D. RAMSAY,
ranging along the Brompton-road, opposite York-place, Queen's
Elms, and near to the Turnpike,
AN UNRIVALLED STOCK OF
STANDARD AND DWARF ROSES,
including most of the newest varieties, exceeding in number 200,000,
among which are white, blush, scarlet, and perpetual Mosses, Unique
Panaché, Aimer Vivert, Mad. Dupry, Village Maid, Lemarque, Maria,
Leonida, La Biche, Don Juan, Rose Ruga, Double Macartney, Four
Seasons, white, blush, red, and scarlet Belle Fabert, perpetual Scotch,
Queen of Perpetuals, Isle de Bourbon, Bonne Geneviese, striped
Aristides, Mossy de Meaux, La Fayette Jessein, Duc de Berri, and an
infinity of others equally rare, and which have been selected for their
beauty by the proprietor during the last twenty years, and offers an
opportunity never before presented. Also the stock of healthy and
thriving evergreens, and deciduous shrubs, climbing plants, dwarf and
trained fruit trees, of the choicest varieties, including,

Sweet Bay,	Arbor Vitæ,	Laburnum,	Snowberry,
Acuba,	Lavender,	Poplars,	Daphnes,
Laurels,	Privets,	Alders,	Honeysuckles,
Hollies,	Elms,	Acacia,	Guelder Roses,
Box,	Oak,	Sweetbriar,	Sweetbriars,
Red Cedar,	Birch,	Lilacs,	Dogwood, &c.

A collection of climbing and other roses established in pots for
forcing.
The lots will be arranged to contain several varieties, and in quan-
tities to meet the wants of individual purchasers.
The nursery was established by the celebrated author of
CURTIS'S BOTANICAL MAGAZINE,
since which its high fame has continued for the great perfection and
beauty of
THE STOCK OF STANDARD AND OTHER ROSES.
The lease of the nursery, which ranges over nearly ten acres, will
also be submitted to sale.
The stock may now be viewed every Saturday and Monday, and
also the three days prior to the sale: Catalogues may be had at Mr.
Ramsay's Stanhope Nursery, Old Brompton; at the Auction Mart,
City; and at Mr. Phillips's offices, 73, New Bond-street, six days
previous to the sale.

PREVIOUS PAGE: Colourful seed packets arrayed on trade stands have always proved an attracitve allure.

ABOVE: *The Compleat Gardener* was written by Jean le Quintinye, gardener to Louis XIV of France, and published in English by George London and Henry Wise. The original translation was said to be by John Evelyn.

ABOVE RIGHT: The Brompton Park area of London, along with Nine Elms, was still a popular location for nurseries in the first part of the nineteenth century. Roses would have benefited from the smog, which keeps black spot at bay.

OPPOSITE: Plant sellers were a common sight in cities in the eighteenth and nineteenth centuries, with plants either sold or hired by the day or week.

For as long as people have gardened they have needed plants and seeds to garden with. Collecting plants from the wild and swapping seeds and "slips" (or cuttings) with their neighbours was for a long time the only way in which gardeners could obtain stock. The first known list of nursery stock was printed by 1670, and was a list of fruit trees available from Mr Garrle, dwelling at the great Nursery between Spittlefields and White-Chappel, "a very Eminent and Ingenious Nursery-man who can furnish any that desireth with any of the sorts hereafter mentioned, as also with divers other rare and choice Plants". Thanks to the research of the garden historian John Harvey, we know that Mr Garrle was in fact Leonard Gurle (1621–85), who became gardener to the king in 1677, replacing the aptly named John Rose. We do not know how large an area Leonard Gurle devoted to his trees, or what other types of plants he sold, but a contemporary nurseryman, George Ricketts, was said to already have a "large nursery" when he bought an additional three-acre (1.2-hectare) orchard in the 1670s.

Undoubtedly, the largest nursery known in the seventeenth and early eighteenth centuries was that run by George London and Henry Wise at Brompton Park, London. Sprawling across some 50 acres (20 or more hectares) that were later to form the site for – rather aptly – the Natural History and Science Museum complex and the Royal Albert Hall, the Brompton nursery specialized in evergreens and trees for the vast eighteenth-century landscape gardens which London and Wise designed. Henry Wise was official royal gardener to both Queen Anne and King George I and the foremost designer of formal gardens with their avenues, parterres and formal groves. Creating such gardens needed literally thousands of plants and the nurseries grew rich on their sales. Wise recommended to his clients that

NURSERIES AND SEEDSMEN

NURSERIES AND SEEDSMEN

ABOVE: Some plant sellers also acted as jobbing gardeners, hired alongside their plants, and would sell plants to their employers, although there must have been a strong temptation to neglect existing plants to create a market for replacements! Jobbing gardeners had a reputation for drunkenness, which this man seems to share.

they favour evergreens such as box, yew, laurel (*Prunus laurocerasus*) and pyracanthus alongside *Phillyrea* and *Arbutus unedo*. Alert to this "insider dealing", one contemporary commented: "As our great modellers of gardens have their magazines of plants to dispose of, it is very natural for them to tear up all the beautiful plantations and contrive a plan that may most turn to their own profit." The Brompton Park nursery has been estimated as having held up to 10 million plants with a value of £40,000 in 1705. London and Wise were also known for their topiary and clipped work, and they supplied such famous sites as Levens Hall, the maze at Hampton Court (for Queen Anne) and a remarkable sunken garden at Kensington, where yew and variegated holly were clipped into the shapes of crenellations and bastions to give the whole "garden" the appearance of a fortification. The satirist Alexander Pope published a fictional catalogue of topiary work for sale by "an eminent nurseryman", including such delights as "ADAM and Eve in yew; Adam a little shatter'd by the fall of the Tree of knowledge in the great storm; Eve and the Serpent very flourishing"; and "A topping Ben Johnson in Laurel with DIVERSE eminent Modern Poets in Bays, somewhat blighted, to be disposed of a pennyworth." Busy at such prestigious gardens as Castle Howard and Chatsworth, it is unlikely that London and Wise were very bothered by such jibes, but the rising fashion for informal landscape with its wide, open expanses of turf and water

NURSERIES AND SEEDSMEN

were to spell the end of their reign. Plant nurseries did, though, continue to be a hallmark of South Kensington into the nineteenth century.

Most eighteenth-century nurseries were considerably smaller than the 50 acres (20 hectares) occupied by London and Wise (some historians have even suggested that at its peak the nursery occupied 100 acres – 40 hectares) and, despite the work of John Harvey, we know little of their stock or manner of trading. Several nurseries are mentioned in the work of the eccentrically named (and eccentric) garden designer Batty Langley, who wrote *New Principles of Gardening* in 1728. The first Langley refers to is Mr Cox, late of Kew Green, who had raised an improved kind of hotspur pea, and the second Master Hot, who had been responsible, presumably, for the original peas of that name – unless he had been named after his own peas. When he died, Mr Cox was said to have 30,000 plants in his nursery. For evergreens, fruit and forest trees, Langley recommends a Mr Peter Mason at Isleworth (Middlesex). Taken with other evidence, it is obvious that early nurseries were even then favouring the areas to the south and west of London – where the air was fresher and land cheap, whilst still within distance of the great consumer hub (and source of night soil) that was London. Although not in quite the same league as London and Wise, Mr Mason had 115,000 plants, and a black carthorse, presumably used for carting his wares.

London was not the only urban area to attract nurseries. James Clarke traded in Dorking, Surrey, or at least he did until he went bankrupt in 1767; John Berry had 5,000 trees and shrubs at his premises 10 miles (16 kilometres) out of Bristol; and Henry Clark of Barnet (Hertfordshire) appears to have specialized in small trees and evergreens as well as holding several "exotics", as newly discovered and imported plants were termed in the eighteenth century. That trees, shrubs and evergreens formed the major part of nursery holdings throughout the eighteenth century comes as no surprise when the garden fashions of the period are considered, although John Harvey's work indicates an increase in flowering and scented shrubs by the end of the century as well as the appearance of rare and imported plants.

As fashions changed and flowers began again to fill our gardens, seedsmen flourished and nurseries sprang up to cater for the amateur gardener, or the lazy householder content to buy his plants ready-grown. The plant hawker became a common sight on the streets of larger towns, providing plants for both sale and hire. Hiring plants was a way of ensuring a fashionable garden and dinner table without the bother of hiring a jobbing gardener (or doing it yourself). In large towns where soot and smut meant that flowers were often spoilt, the nursery would supply you fresh clean plants and take away the old ones. By the 1840s, Louisa Johnson despaired that the lot of the lady gardener "in large towns, under the influence

ABOVE: Carters' Tested Seed Company was one of the big seed suppliers in the late nineteenth century and continued to lead the market through the twentieth century. Their headquarters at Raynes Park in London was planted up with decorative vegetables during the Second World War.

BELOW: Florists' societies, with a membership comprised of amateur collectors and breeders of the established "florists' flowers" (carnations, ranunculus, tulips etc), were the obvious focus for the improvement of varieties.

At a Florist Feast held at the King's Arms in Lambeth Marsh, a few Days since, there was a Carnation Flower produced, which was greatly esteemed for its Perfection and Beauty, for which Reason it was unanimously agreed that the most consistent Name to be given to the same was, "Lord Chief Justice Pratt," which was accordingly done, to the Satisfaction of all present. *July 18 1764*

RIGHT: A wealth of information on planting is available from seedsmen's invoices and bills. Unofrtunately many are almost illegible!

BELOW: The Miller nurseries traded in Bristol from about 1786 under various combinations of Miller & Sweet, Sweets & Miller and finally John Miller (1824–37). Despite having an attractive tradecard, Miller went bankrupt in 1837, although the actual business was taken over as a going concern by James Garaway. In 1822 Miller was described by the garden writer John Claudius Loudon as "the most extensive garden-tradesman in the west of England".

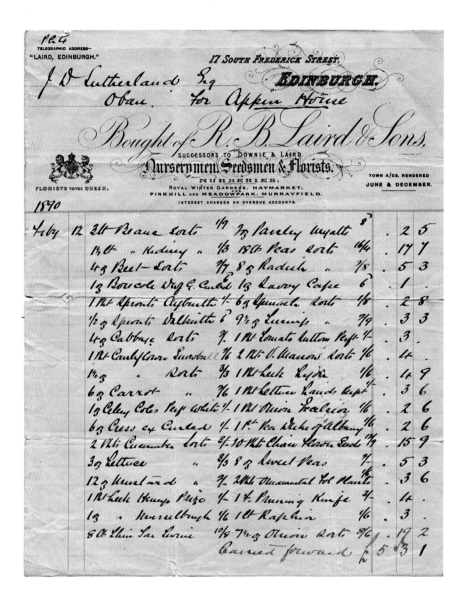

of coal smoke, shade and gloom ... will be constant disappointment" as "she can only hope to keep a few consumptive geraniums languishing through the summer months, to die in October, and show the desolating views of rows of pots containing blackened and dusty stems". As London smogs worsened, the nursery trade bloomed.

Some nurserymen became famous for introducing a new variety, or coaxing an exotic foreign introduction into flower for the first time: Thomas Fairchild, on the other hand, revolutionized our understanding of how plants change and new species develop. At a meeting of the Royal Society in February 1720, Fairchild announced that he had "discovered" a new species. A cross between a carnation and a sweet william, the plant had supposedly been found growing in a spot at Fairchild's Hoxton nursery where the seeds of these

NURSERIES AND SEEDSMEN

two other species had "accidentally" been scattered. In fact, Fairchild was well known for trying to improve the flowers in his care, and was also a close friend of Thomas Knowlton, who was investigating the possible sexual nature of plant reproduction. Suggesting that plants had a sex life was bad enough, but interfering with that sexual congress to produce a totally new species was seen as positively blasphemous in the eighteenth century – and so Fairchild fell back on the ploy of suggesting that the whole thing had been an accident of nature. The plant he shyly took from his pocket that cold February night (pressed and preserved from the previous summer) became known as Fairchild's mule – as, in common with most hybrids, including the famous cross between the horse and donkey, it was not capable of further reproduction. As the Royal Society heard, Fairchild's friend Knowlton had also "found" a very similar plant growing between his sweet williams and carnations at Offley Place (Hertfordshire), where he worked as a gardener. Whatever the truth of the story, Fairchild's mule was officially the first "bastard flower" (as the eighteenth-century Fellows phrased it), and Fairchild's nursery earned a place in history. Hybridization, however, still had a long struggle ahead of it before it was widely acknowledged as a horticultural tool. Well into the nineteenth century, nurserymen were afraid to exhibit hybrids at horticultural society shows, fearing that they would be accused of being irreligious. Instead, they showed flowers of improved colour and size produced by selective breeding, or so they said.

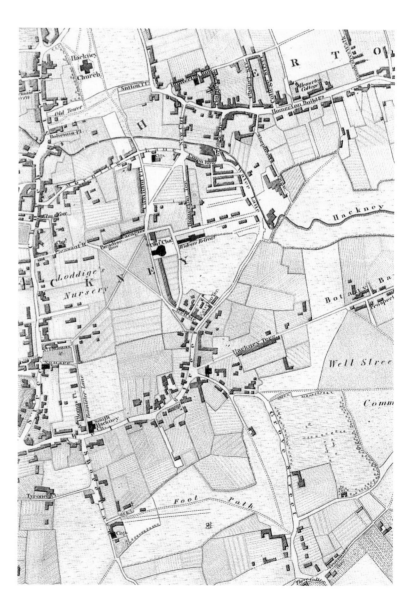

BELOW: Loddiges famous nursery as shown on the Greenwood Map of London in 1827. The map shows the scale of the nursery at its height, and its semi-rural location in Hackney.

The early nineteenth century saw the birth of many family seed and nursery businesses that continued to bloom well into the twentieth and even the twenty-first centuries. Robinson's Seeds & Plants, now known as the "Home of the Giant Onion" and specializing in vegetable seeds for show, was founded in 1860 by William Robinson (no relation to the garden designer of the same name). Originally established as a nursery, Robinson's grew bush and tree fruit as well as a full range of vegetables and the onions and leeks that were to become a hallmark of the company. A range of glasshouses spread across the 22-acre (nine-hectare) site, with cows and horses also being kept for manure and traction. It was William Robinson's son (also William!) who began to specialize in the "mammoth" onions and leeks that gained the company show success and renown into the 1930s and again after the war, under the third generation,

ABOVE: Brunton, Forbes and Hunter traded in Birmingham during 1787–97, although Brunton appears to have set up initially in 1777. Many early seedsmen and nurserymen appear to have had rapid changes of partners, often starting as one-man concerns.

William Martin Robinson. Robinson's Mammoth Onions still make an appearance at the RHS Chelsea Flower Show, and onions of over 4.4 pounds (two kilograms) have won prizes around the country from the late 1800s.

Worldwide fame awaited some of the Victorian nurserymen who ventured into exotics and plant hunting. Veitch's, originally founded by John Veitch some time before 1808, had businesses in Exeter and Chelsea by the middle of the century – using a base in Devon for the breeding of tender exotics brought in to the south coast docks. Veitch's was the first commercial nursery to send its own plant collectors round the world with instructions to collect specific plants. Other nurseries used freelance collectors to look for "anything of interest". Veitch's often trained local men in plant identification and collection at their own nurseries before sending them out to the uncharted territories of the Himalayas, Japan and China. By 1914, the family-run nursery had introduced 1,281 plants into England, either as importations or newly bred varieties. These included 498 greenhouse plants, 232 orchids, 153 deciduous trees and shrubs, and 118 exotic ferns – to cater for the fern craze. Amongst those sent across the world by the nursery were the brothers William and Thomas Lobb (William to South and North America, Thomas to the Far East); Ernest "Chinese" Wilson, who collected the handkerchief or dove tree (*Davidia involucrata*); and Charles Maries. Harry Veitch was renowned for keeping tight control of his collectors and advised the then relatively inexperienced Ernest Wilson that he should "Stick to the one thing you are after and don't spend time and money wandering about. Probably every worthwhile plant in China has now been introduced to Europe." Just for once Harry Veitch was wrong, and Ernest Wilson spent a lifetime discovering more, including the *Lilum regale* and the *Actinidia deliciosa* (better known as the kiwi fruit). Thanks to their intrepid plant hunters, Veitch's nursery transformed the English landscape garden with avenues of *Sequoiadendron giganteum* (Wellingtonia), bristling monkey puzzle trees and hothouses full of exotic orchids.

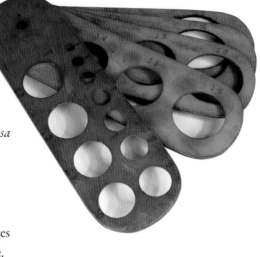

Competing for the Victorian gardener's attention and purse was the Loddiges nursery. This, too was, a family affair whose eventual fame was to be worldwide. The family originated in Germany (the Veitch family had originally come from Scotland) with the surname Lochlies, which in common with many emigrants they anglicized so as to "fit in". Trading in exotic seeds was an essential part of the small business founded by Conrad Loddiges with his fellow German emigré John Busch in the late 1770s. By the simple expedient of writing to people in different countries and asking them to send him seeds, Conrad established a name for rare and unusual plants. By the early nineteenth century, the nursery was well established under George Loddiges, who published 2,000 coloured pictures of rare plants housed in the Loddiges hothouses and gardens. Many of these had been first imported using the newly invented Wardian case, which sealed in the atmosphere and allowed plants to make long sea crossings without being affected by sea spray and lack of fresh water. Loddiges nursery was based in Hackney, then further from the dense and polluted heart of London than it is now. The nursery and associated arboretum attracted botanists and scientists who were fascinated by the work the nursery carried out "improving" the plants in its care. Charles Darwin visited in 1838 and noted that he "saw in Loddiges garden 1279 varieties of roses!!! Proof of capability of variation." George Loddiges received numerous awards and medals from the Horticultural Society (not then Royal) including the Sir Joseph Banks Memorial Portrait Prize in 1823 and the President's Silver Medal in 1836. The nursery closed in 1854 when St Thomas' Hospital, the owners of the land on which the nursery was sited, raised the rent, forcing the then owner, Conrad Loddiges (II), to look (unsuccessfully) for other premises. The stock was offered to Kew Gardens as a single lot, but this was refused and the collection was broken up, with some being purchased by Joseph Paxton for the newly built Crystal Palace. Amongst the many exotic plants introduced by Loddiges, there is one which now strikes fear into many a garden historian's heart – the *Rhododendron ponticum*, or "common" mauve rhododendron, which from its first introduction by Conrad Loddiges in the 1760s has literally overwhelmed much of the English landscape.

Whilst nurseries were often set up by entrepreneurial gardeners, such as the young John Veitch, seed companies were commonly an offshoot of corn

ABOVE: A bulb sorter as used by nurseries for grading and sorting.

BELOW: These seed-measuring spoons were the property of Lake & McKenzie Ltd of Liverpool.

ABOVE: Elphicks seed sellers used this album of collected cuttings to show their customers the various plants available and how to grow them.

BELOW: Sorting and counting seeds was carried out using seed sorters such as this sweet pea sorter, which could hold 50 seeds.

and grain merchants – both needing the same sort of storage and handling – or of general hardware retailers. Sutton's Seeds was originally established in 1806 by John Sutton under the original name of "House of Sutton" as a corn merchant. It was not until 1837 that the Reading-based company, by then including his sons, Martin Hope Sutton and Alfred Sutton, branched out into vegetable and flower seeds. In 1840, they established in-house seed-testing laboratories and nursery trial grounds so that they could verify claims for purity and germination rates. Success for the company was marked by royal patronage and from 1858 it could boast "By Appointment" with a Royal Warrant from Queen Victoria. The coming of the railway to Reading resulted in the expansion of the business as wholesale and smaller orders could be transported cheaply around the country, reaching the amateur gardener and country estate alike. By 1873, expanded offices, stables, testing grounds and exhibition departments (and even a private fire station) formed part of the

NURSERIES AND SEEDSMEN

successful business. As an independent seed supplier Sutton's survived into the 1990s, before becoming part of the much larger international Vilmorin company, although the seed packets are still comfortably labelled "Sutton's".

Cuthbert's seeds, which celebrated its 200-year anniversary in 1997, was established as part of a general trading store by James Cuthbert, originally from Scotland, as were so many eighteenth- and nineteenth-century gardeners and horticulturalists. He set up a landscaping and general supplies service in Southgate, then in the rural hinterland of London, where he supplied such necessities as servant's livery, tea and gunpowder. However, the garden services led his sons to concentrate on growing plants and supplying fruit trees and bushes, which were later joined, when fashions changed, by flowering garden shrubs and camellias. Seeds and bulbs formed part of the business, but it was a deal with F W Woolworth, the popular general store, in 1937, that pushed Cuthbert's seed packets to the forefront. The outbreak of war and the Dig for

ABOVE: Before the war, many flower bulbs came from Holland. During the war what home production there was had to be sent to America to try and raise money in return for munitions and food supplies, especially bread wheat.

LEFT: This Sutton's catalogue captures the start of the fashion for Japanese and Chinese garden design, although nurseries such as Veitch's were responsible for sending out the plant hunters to those countries.

ABOVE: Onions were one of the first casualties of war. In 1938 over 90 per cent had been imported from France and Spain; by Christmas 1940 they were so precious that people gave them as presents. This is an unusually colourful wartime image.

ABOVE RIGHT: Cuthbert's popular seeds sold through Woolworth branches.

BELOW: Carters' 1941 catalogue echoed the austere mood of the times, with food production a priority and even paper in short supply.

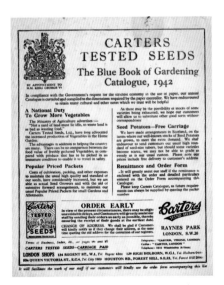

Victory campaign meant that demand outstripped supply, as all aspects of the Cuthbert's business became focused on the nation's attempts to grow its own food. The popularity of Woolworth and the fashion for brightly coloured annuals combined to make the 1950s a similar success, and Clay Jones, later to have a media career on the radio programme *Gardeners' Question Time*, was employed to tour the Woolworth counters, checking on stock and giving crash courses in horticulture to the shop staff, whom he named "hortigirls".

Not many businesses start on an allotment, but Gandy's Roses has come a long way from its distinctly humble beginnings to its present company motto "The Connoisseur's Choice". Douglas Gandy rented his first allotment shortly after the family moved from Kent to South Kilworth (Leicestershire) in the 1920s. By 1925, he was concentrating on rose growing, catering for the most popular of inter-war plants. As his business grew and the general demand for allotments fell, he took over more allotments until he eventually occupied the whole of the village allotment field. By the early 1930s, when Gandy started to employ other people, he was growing 30–40,000 roses a year and sending them (bare-rooted) around the country, using the local rail station. War brought disaster, as it did for so many nurseries. By then, Gandy had moved to premises in North Kilworth. The nursery came under government regulation and Gandy was forced to sell up most of his stock, including unique varieties, and convert to food production. Obviously not happy amidst brassicas and beans, he was reported for growing strawberries, a crop not sanctioned by the Ministry of Agriculture, and threatened with imprisonment if these were not replaced by cabbages within the fortnight. Rose breeders were particularly badly hit by the Second World War, with stock having to be uprooted, and many of the varieties bred in the 1930s were lost. Afterwards, the nurseries looked to Europe and

America for restocking. The famous Peace rose introduced in 1948 by Gandy's rival, Wheatcroft Rose Nursery, was brought from France.

The Second World War brought its own problems for nurseries and seed merchants. Although vegetable seeds experienced a massive demand, many suppliers were simply not in a position to benefit from this, whilst those who specialized in hothouse plants, flowering bulbs, decorative shrubs and trees, or traded in plants supplied from abroad, faced ruin. Supplies were cut off, rare collections summarily disposed of, and up to 90 per cent of the stock of any

BELOW: The Yates company, founded in Manchester in 1826, entered the Australasian market in the 1880s. In 1916, as the Great War raged in Europe, the company's Tasmanian flower farm on the Derwent River was established.

RIGHT: This wonderfully decorated seed tin contained a selection of Sutton's most popular flower seeds from the 1920s.

OPPOISTE TOP: Wheatcroft of Nottingham, fronted by the flamboyant Harry Wheatcroft, was the most famous rose nursery through the 1950s and '60s. Harry was said to have brought sex to the garden industry and was often seen with an open-fronted shirt and a bevy of beautiful young women.

nursery ploughed in or uprooted to make way for the growing of foodstuffs or seed supply. In December 1940, St John's Nursery (Sevenoaks, Kent) held a clearance sale of stock in order to clear its land for food growing. The stock included 20,000 roses of all kinds and 5,000 fruit trees. Mr S J Miles, a commercial carnation grower from Bayham Abbey gardens, was also forced to adapt rapidly, and turned his carnation nurseries to tomato growing, even writing an article about his success under the rather misleading title of "The War-time Cultivation of Carnations". As the war progressed, paper shortages resulted in seed and plant catalogues being restricted, and by 1944 these

A PLEA TO "CONTINUE AS NORMAL" DURING WARTIME

"The Council of the Royal Horticultural Society … draws the attention of Fellows of the Society and of the public to the desirability of continuing to place orders with nurserymen. If orders are absent very much of the work that nurserymen have done during the past few years will be wasted. Moreover, it would be a calamity if, owing to the scarcity of orders, many of them were compelled to close their businesses entirely, for unless some stock is retained during the war it will be many years after the cessation of hostilities before they will be again in a position to play their essential part in the horticultural life of the country. It is hoped that these points will be kept in mind by all amateur gardeners and that orders for trees, shrubs and other plants will not be discontinued unless this is found to be absolutely necessary."

The Gardeners' Chronicle, *September 1939*

NURSERIES AND SEEDSMEN

had been reduced to a list of seeds with few or no images. Catalogues of vegetable seeds were usually provided free, to encourage the Dig for Victory campaign, but flower-seed catalogues had to be sent for and paid for – further discouraging purchases. Many nurseries simply went out of business and the pages of *The Gardeners' Chronicle* for the war years testifies to this, with the frequency of advertisements for "all remaining stock and glasshousing to be sold at auction". Labour shortages, conscription and even bombing (the London warehouse of Hurst & Sons was hit in 1941, and many others had glasshouses shattered) all resulted in many small suppliers closing during the war years, and the intensely harsh winter and spring of 1946–47 finished off others.

Some larger seed companies such as Webbs, Ryders', Carters' and Sutton's were well placed to survive the war years, and in fact expand as demand for vegetable seeds grew. In spring 1941, Webbs was offering its "popular collection of vegetable seeds" packaged as an "ideal assortment for the 10-pole plot". At only five shillings each, these were guaranteed to ensure a plentiful supply of fresh vegetables through the year.

WATERERS FLORAL MILE
over 200 acres of Nursery Stock—embracing Herbaceous Plants, Irises, Alpines, Fruit Trees—and over 250,000 Roses

DISPLAY GARDEN

We have established at our Floral Mile Nursery an attractive Display Garden covering an area of more than 2 acres.
Numerous beds of Floribunda and Hybrd Tea Roses, Bearded Irises, Phlox, Lupins, Michaelmas Daisies, Chrysanthemums, Dahlias, etc. have been planted to give flower throughout the season.
These beds are interspersed with wide grass paths leading to a Rock Garden and well planned Shrub and Herbaceous Borders.
This feature gives a wonderful opportunity for our customers to see a wide range of plants flowering in their natural setting and will prove of great assistance in choosing desirable subjects for garden culture.
EVERY PLANT IS DISTINCTLY LABELLED—THERE IS PLENTY OF ROOM TO WALK ROUND

GARDEN CENTRES

At both the Floral Mile, Twyford and at our Tree & Shrub Nursery at Bagshot, Surrey, we have a special department well-stocked with a large selection of Shrubs, Roses, Fruit, Climbing Plants, Conifers, Bedding Plants, Alpines, etc.—in season—available for "CASH & CARRY" sale.

ABOVE: Rivers of Sawbridgeworth (Hertfordshire) was another family business, originally founded in 1725. Thomas Rivers (1797–1877) made the nurseries famous by inventing glasshousing for fruit trees. Thomas Francis Rivers (1831–99) was responsible for the development of the Conference pear. The nursery finally closed in 1985.

LEFT: The new garden centres revolutionized plant buying.

10

Gnome from Gnome: Suburbia in the 1950s and '60s

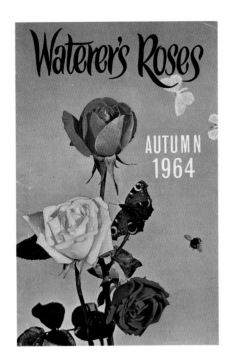

PREVIOUS PAGE: Making the most of urban space was vital in the 1950s and '60s. This image by Ronald Lampitt celebrates the ingenuity of urban gardeners.

ABOVE: Hybrid teas and standard roses in technicolour yellows and reds were a hallmark of the 1960s garden. Waterer's nursery was later taken over by Notcutts.

ABOVE MIDDLE: The end of the war did not spell the end of rationing, and vegetable growing was still popular throughout the austerity years. Ryders' continued to offer its "Famous V Collection" alongside its flower selection.

ABOVE RIGHT: Coronation year was another opportunity for nurseries to celebrate the return of flowers into the garden, and many published commemorative seed and plant lists.

As Britain struggled to feed itself in the post-war austerity years, there was, at first, little celebration in the garden. Flowers had been allowed to creep back in and lawns reinstated, but for many householders there was neither the time nor the inclination to replant the magnificent flower borders of the inter-war years. Annuals were the order of the day for many suburban gardens, perhaps resulting from a lingering doubt that it really was all over. Neat rows of busy lizzie (*impatiens*) and antirrhinum displayed as much earth as colour and could be cultivated in the same way as vegetables: seeded in spring, pricked out, and then harvested in the autumn. Low maintenance and low cost, they were ideal for bringing almost instant colour to thousands of post-war prefabs and the council housing which sprung up in the wake of the New Towns Act of 1946 and the Town and Country Planning Act of 1947. Small gardens at the front, not yet occupied by car parking, necessitated a handkerchief-size lawn and a ribbon of earth, whilst the back garden often still harboured a vegetable patch, "just in case".

Pride of place in many of these gardens, alongside the home-made birdbaths and sundials, went to perhaps the most famous rose ever: Peace. This was a yellow hybrid tea-rose which had its origins in France. It had supposedly been sent to the United States on the last plane leaving before the German invasion, and once there it was cultivated by the famous Conard-Pyle Co. After the war, the same rose was imported into England by the flamboyant Harry Wheatcroft. The Wheatcroft brothers, Harry and Alfred, had lost almost all their original rose stock during the war, but by using European connections came to dominate post-war rose gardens with their brightly colour hybrid teas, which captured the mood of the nation with names such as Super Star, Fragrant Cupid and Queen Elizabeth, the latter in honour of the 1953 Coronation.

Less cautious than the average gardener, the government had decided to celebrate the end of austerity early with the promotion of a festival of the visual arts, giving a new identity of modernism and progressiveness to weary, war-torn Britain. The Festival of Britain would be a "tonic to the nation", focusing on the best of British design and industry. The festival encompassed exhibitions and events all over the country, but it was the main South Bank site in London that was to prove most influential for architects and landscape designers. Drawing on the new wave of modernist sculpture and extensive use of concrete, the festival organizers provided a riverside setting for its Pavilion of Homes

ABOVE: Garden gnomes, first popularized in the nineteenth century, made a bid for the suburbs after their reincarnation as Disney dwarves in the late 1940s. Some gardens even boasted the full set of seven dwarves, complete with Snow White!

LEFT: The Festival of Britain included the glorious Battersea Park Pleasure Gardens replete with big dipper, dance pavilions, theatre and flower beds. Austerity had no place in such a post-war paradise.

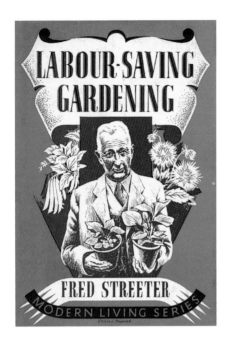

ABOVE: "Labour-saving" was the gardening catch phrase of the austerity-hit 1950s and, despite increased leisure time, the 1960s continued the theme as television competed with traditional leisure activities.

BELOW: DDT was to be the post-war answer to the gardener's dreams, killing pests of all kinds with very little effort. Soon the dream turned to nightmare.

and Gardens, complete with moated "garden", murals and sculpture. Inspired and in turn inspiring, it provided a model for public spaces in New Towns like Harlow and Milton Keynes which included the work of designers such as Frank Gibberd and Sylvia Crowe (the latter originally trained at Swanley Horticultural College). More to the taste of many visitors than the concrete setting of the festival, however, were the Festival Pleasure Gardens, created on the south side of the Thames, at Battersea Park. Here fountains played, planters bloomed and fairground rides whirled people into a more comfortingly ornate future of gilded luxury.

Struggling to resurrect the glory of the garden from the combined impact of war and austerity, many gardeners took up the rallying cry of the "labour-saving garden". Labour of all forms was in short supply in the post-war years, and householders who in the past would have employed at least a cleaner or jobbing gardener found themselves tackling all the household and garden chores on their own. Larger country houses and country-house gardens were also hard hit as the traditional life "in service" became unpopular. Many estates went into public hands, where cost cutting was demanded by new controllers. As Richard Sudell summed up in 1952:

> The modern large garden is ... the garden maintained by a public authority, and whatever the position of labour supply, economy in its upkeep must be practised. Even the smallest garden also has its labour problem, for although hours of work are perhaps shorter now than ever before, there are far more calls on the leisure hours of the average man. And between the owner of a small garden plot, torn between the desire to make a good little garden and the wish to make the most of his television set, and the controller of the large estate who must report favourably on finances to his committee, there exist a multitude of garden owners who are all faced with the same problem – not enough man-hours.

Fortunately, as Sudell pointed out, the war that had caused these problems had also resulted in numerous inventions of practical use in the garden, and those, plus some adjustment of design, meant time and money could be saved. The labour-saving garden was born.

A motor-mower was the first essential to the anxious time-strapped gardener, and one especially recommended where lawns were over a quarter of an acre (a

	5% **D.D.T. DUST** Kills Pea and Bean Weevil, Carrot and Onion Fly, Cabbage Caterpillars, Wasps, Flea Beetle, etc.	Sprinkler carton 2 lb. tins	2 doz. 8 tins
	BABY " PUFFIT "	Polythene Dispenser	2 doz.
	LARGE " PUFFIT " ... ... Refillable	Polythene Dispenser	1 doz.

tenth of a hectare). The paving of smaller gardens might dispense with mowing altogether, and could be conveniently combined with the advent of the outdoor eating room, as Mediterranean habits infiltrated Britain. Electric hedge-clippers achieved the work of a day in less than an hour, although for true labour saving the wise gardener dispensed with hedging entirely. Shrubs triumphed over bedding, although only if they grew slowly and compactly, needing little pruning or management. Self-clinging climbing plants could be used to cover large expanses of brickwork and, despite its often untidy habit, climbing knotweed (*Polygonum baldschuanicum*) gained a foothold in the garden (to be followed undoubtedly by numerous toeholds!). Strawberrries, that delight of the English summer, were considered by Sudell as being "very demanding over labour" and best replaced with an apple or pear tree. Simplicity was a keynote; "a strip of lawn with a few evergreen and flowering shrubs and trees" with perhaps a couple of tubs of bright flowers was all that was needed in a front garden, whilst a small back garden could be transformed into an open paved space with surrounding border. Berberis, ceanothus, euonymus and pieris became the foot soldiers in the battle against time-wasting, supported by a battalion of "non-living features".

Gardeners who insisted on having some growing plants in their garden could also benefit from advances in science and technology through the enthusiastic use of weed-killers and pesticides. Selective weed-killer, which affected broad-leaved plants but not grass, revolutionized lawn care in the 1950s and '60s, whilst the more general availability of DDT held out a vision for a pest-free world in an era when the word "biodiversity" would have had most gardeners reaching for their sprayer.

BELOW: "Concrete is perhaps the most useful of all materials in a small garden." Richard Sudell, *The Labour Saving Garden* (1952)

BOTTOM LEFT: A garden by the designer Geoffrey Jellicoe at Wexham Springs (Buckinghamshire). Jellicoe successfully combined elements of classical and modern design in the post-war period, and was a founding member of the Institute of Landscape Architects alongside Brenda Colvin .

BOTTOM RIGHT: A typical outdoor room with the substantial pergola acting as roof and wall.

Two Steps ahead in the Garden with **JEYES**

Architectural features were to be the meeting-point of modernism and labour saving. Concrete pergolas, paved patios, walls, rills and terraces all proclaimed a weed-free future of television-watching for the gardener who had planned carefully at the outset. For those who still had domestic staff, a paved garden area was also recommended for their enjoyment! Concrete was not the only non-living material recommended for the garden. In John Brooke's 1968 *Room Outside: A Plan for the Garden*, over 30 pages were dedicated to "hard surfacing", including tarmacadam, asphalt, brick, stone slabs, gravel and pre-cast slabs. A further four pages dwelt on walling, and ten more on garden furnishings (chairs, barbecues, urns, pots, sculpture and statues). The outdoor room (as opposed to a garden designed as "garden rooms") caught on in an age of increased foreign travel and holidays on the Costa. For garden designers such as John Brookes its inspiration was not cheap holidays but was embedded in "a new form of garden thinking" growing out of a longer evolution of garden history. Designers looked to the United States and Scandinavia for this architectural style, which was "brought together and tried out with newly emerging building styles at the Festival of Britain in 1951".

ABOVE: Jeyes Fluid was once regarded as a catch-all for everything in the garden, from sterilizing soil, destroying pests, cleaning concrete and treating rose black spot. Gardeners might have been less keen had they read the recommendations to "leave for six weeks before replanting". Since 2003, Jeyes Fluid has not been licensed for use in the garden.

OPPOSITE: Woolworth stores continued to sell seeds, tools and garden sundries, competing with the popular out-of-town garden centres. Plantoids were another labour-saving idea, allowing easy feeding of plants, along with automatic garden sprinklers.

Design did not always sit easily with horticulture, and even less so with the type of hobby gardening most people indulged in on a sunny Sunday afternoon. Soon, the ways were parting between landscape designers and gardeners, just as they had for a while in the nineteenth century. John Ernest Grant White, himself from a long line of garden designers, commented despairingly: "Undoubtedly there is to be found in this country a natural flair and enthusiasm for cultivating the big variety of ornamental trees and plants which our versatile climate favours, but let us realize at the outset that there is a very real difference and distinction between an imposing show of flowers and a well-designed garden, and it is failure to appreciate this fact that so often leads to disappointment." In his *Designing a Garden Today*, published in 1966, Grant White opined that so many of the gardens of the period were, from a landscape architect's point of view, a terrible waste of time and money, being simply a bewildering mass of bloom masking a poverty of design. Women, he claimed, were particularly at fault, having no clear plan in mind when they started their garden and a tendency towards focusing on plants rather than design.

ABOVE: Even the most colourful lawnmower still needed someone to push it!

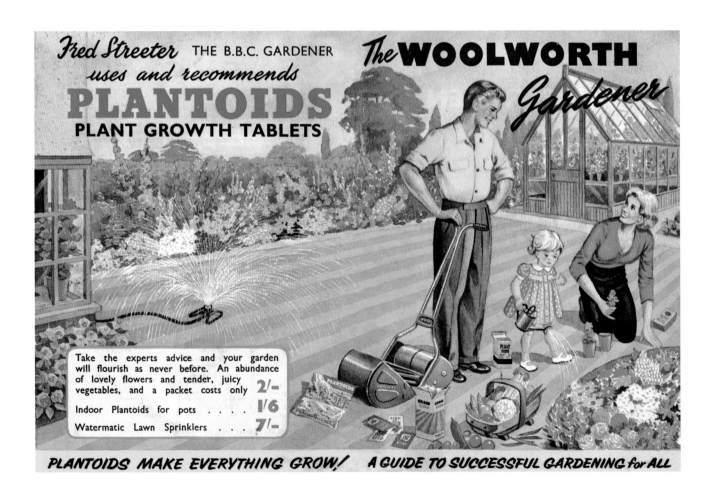

BE YOUR OWN
GARDENING EXPERT

BY DR. D. G. HESSAYON

This invaluable book tells you in plain language all you need to know about improving your soil, understanding the needs of your plants, and recognising and dealing with the pests and diseases that attack them. It is full of answers to questions you have so often asked and never been able to find answered in ordinary gardening books.

1'6

FREE
SOIL TESTER
INSIDE!

LEFT: An early edition of *Be Your Own Gardening Expert.* Colourful and easy to use, the Expert guides were to sell over 50 million copies in the following 50 years.

OPPOSITE: House plants, including the ubiquitous spider plant, were to become a hallmark of 1960s and 1970s interior design. *Be Your Own House Plant Expert* was soon on the bookshelf of every newlywed.

As gardening became allied with decorating, designing and creating instant outdoor rooms, so the market in ready-potted plants and gardening accessories boomed. Rather than going to a nursery for bare-rooted plants, a seedsman for seeds and a stonemason for paving, gardeners wanted to be able to visit just one place for all their needs – from tools to trellises. The concept of the "garden centre", born in America, did not arrive in England until the mid-1950s. In 1953, the then managing director of Waterer's Nurseries returned from a trip to America with the seeds of this revolution. His inspiration resulted in a show stall at Chelsea where plants were shown growing in containers, complete with labels telling you how to grow them and when they would flower. Waterer's would later be taken over by Notcutts, themselves early on the scene with a garden centre built in 1958 on the side of their existing nursery in Woodbridge and including a "planteria". Stewarts Garden Centre in Ferndown, Dorset,

OPPOSITE: Auto-controlled lawnmowers were still a distant dream in the 1950s (from Fred Streeter, *Labour-Saving Gardening*).

converted from its original nursery roots by Edward Stewart in 1955, also underwent a similar transformation, this time inspired by a business trip to Toronto. Although not the first garden centre, the Stewarts' expanded premises, built on a site in Christchurch in 1961, was the first to boast an on-site café. Purchasing plants already in bloom meant that novice gardeners had an idea of what they would look like in their garden, taking the worry out of buying bare-rooted plants out of season and having to wait six months before finding out whether you had ordered the right plant from the mass of Latin names in the nursery catalogue. Visiting a garden centre quickly became a popular weekend activity, perhaps even more popular than gardening itself, and thousands of visitors returned with "instant gardens" bulging from their car boots.

With a new generation of post-war amateur gardeners, the hunt was on for cheap-and-cheerful gardening manuals that captured the feel of the post-war garden and ousted the older-style publications still being re-issued from the war years. First published in 1958, *Be Your Own Gardening Expert* by Dr

CATALOGUE

THE MARGERY FISH NURSERY
EAST LAMBROOK MANOR
SOUTH PETHERTON
SOMERSET
South Petherton 328

Hessayon revolutionized gardening manuals. Gone were pictures of men in braces and flat caps and admonitions to order onion seed early; instead spry women, capably pruning roses, chose shrubs from a multitude available at their local garden centres, whilst their husbands installed electric heating in glasshouses. *Be Your Own Gardening Expert* was followed by Dr Hessayon's "Expert" books on nearly every aspect of the garden, from the lawn to the vegetable plot. The Experts even followed the gardener indoors to help them with their house plants and flower arranging. The books were translated into over 22 different languages, gaining their author a Lifetime Achievement in the British Book Awards as well as a Veitch Memorial medal from the RHS and a Guinness World Records certificate for the best-selling non-fiction author of the 1990s. Fifty years after its first publication, the Experts series had sold 50 million copies and was still adding to its titles with *The Green Garden Expert* – a testament to the success of the 1950s vision.

Not all gardeners wanted to embrace a brave new world of concreted outdoor living and modernist architecture, or even a suburban fantasy of colour. For those whose gardening style harkened back more to the nineteenth-century cottage than the twentieth-century semi, the writings of Margery Fish came as manna from heaven. Margery and her husband Walter had moved into their Somerset cottage in 1937, fearing the imminent outbreak of war and its effect on their London lives. Walter was a gardener of the "old school", for whom chrysanthemums marched in rows, lawns had stripes and gravel rolling

ABOVE LEFT: Responsible for the 1950s revival of the "cottage garden" style, Margery Fish took her inspiration from earlier writers such as William Robinson.

ABOVE: In the mid-1950s, Margery Fish established the nursery at her home in East Lambrook (Somerset) in response to requests for plants she mentioned in her popular books.

was a fine art. Margery, however, enthused over the "cottage garden" style, using traditional hardy plants set in "a good bone structure" of evergreen planting to create a year-round garden. Labour saving was not a part of Margery's gardening mantra and she eschewed instant bedding or seasonal quick-fixes. Appealing to the middle classes whom the war had left with gardens but no money for gardeners, Margery wrote, "It is pleasant to know each one of your plants intimately because you have chosen and planted every one of them." Embarking on the gardens at East Lambrook Manor with, as Grant White might have adversely commented, a greater love of plants than commitment to landscape design, it was no wonder that Margery Fish's greatest contribution was to be the re-establishment of traditional "cottage" style plants, albeit many of improved varieties. Establishing her own nursery, she specialized in hardy

MAKING A GARDEN

"Gardening is like everything else in life, you get out of it as much as you put in. No one can make a garden by buying a few packets of seeds or doing an afternoon's weeding. You must love it, and then your love will be repaid a thousandfold, as every gardener knows."

Margery Fish, We Made A Garden, *1956*

LEFT: A pathway at East Lambrook Manor Gardens which shows the cottage-garden style of planting which the gardens' owner, Margery Fish championed.

GARDENING GURU: PERCY THROWER

With the coming of television came the rise of the media gardener. Born into a family of gardeners, with his father head gardener at Horwood House (Buckinghamshire), Percy Thrower was one of the last of the old school. Starting work at Horwood House at the age of 14, he became a journeyman gardener four years later, travelling to gain experience in all areas of garden work. Living in the "bothy" at Windsor Castle on a £1 a week wage, his experiences were little different to those of the Victorians who had come before him. A move to Sandringham saw him married in 1939 to the head gardener's daughter; the couple received a wedding gift of china from Queen Mary. As Parks Superintendent at Derby, he was later active in the Dig for Victory campaign. Thrower first appeared on television in 1951 to talk about a garden he had designed in Germany. His enthusiasm and self-assured manner made him a natural, with regular gardening spots in everything from *Out and About* (later renamed *Gardeners' World*) to *Blue Peter* — on which he established a children's gardening slot from 1974 until 1987. His spell at *Gardeners' World* ended in 1976 when he signed a contract with Plant Products (ICI) for a series of commercials, but he continued to have immense influence over amateur gardening through his writings in newspapers and gardening magazines. In 1973, he was awarded the prestigious RHS Victoria Medal of Honour, and in 1984 was further recognized with an MBE. His own garden, at The Magnolias, Shrewsbury (Shropshire), was regularly thrown open to raise money for charity and he continued to garden despite the onset of Hodgkin's disease; his last appearance on *Blue Peter* was made just a week before his death in 1988.

geraniums and other trouble-free plants which rewarded the gardener who learnt their preferences for shade or sun, dry or wet. Margery herself was rewarded by having numerous garden essentials named after her, including *Penstemon* "Margery Fish" and the very useful *Pulmonaria* "Margery Fish" with its sharply-pointed spotted leaves and its pink to blue tubular flowers.

As the achievements of the Women's Land Army faded into memory, women were left uneasily straddling their traditional roles in the house and the world of work. The "brave new world" of vacuum cleaners, washing machines and crease-free fabrics liberated them from much of the drudgery, but often left them with few alternative occupations. Well into the 1960s, women were expected to leave their jobs once they married and had children, often never to return. In the hours between Tupperware parties and "Avon Calling", the 1960s housewife discovered flower arranging and with it the flower-arranger's garden. Constance Spry was the doyenne of the flower-arranging world. Originally a nurse and then a headmistress at a day school for adults, she championed flower arranging for the

ABOVE: The fashion for enjoying the outside inside resulted in thousands of DIY "sun lounges" being tacked on to houses. Often of flimsy construction, these were replaced with a wave of UPVC conservatories in the 1990s.

working and middle classes in the 1930s, when flower decorating was the preserve of the wealthy: by 1934, she employed 70 people at her shop in Pimlico. But for most housewives her major impact was to be in the post-war period, when leisure and home ownership transformed domestic duties to include the decoration and presentation of the house and dinner table. *How To Do The Flowers*, published in 1952, was soon on everyone's bookshelves, and no dinner party was complete without an artfully themed arrangement. Her influence on the domestic sphere was wide ranging, especially after she opened a school of Domestic Science with her friend Rosemary Hume shortly after the war. It was Constance Spry who arranged the flowers at Westminster and Buckingham Palace to celebrate the Coronation of Queen Elizabeth II, and Hume who created the dish of the decade, "Coronation Chicken", served at a meal for foreign delegates who attended. One of the keys to Constance Spry's success was her emphasis on easily available plants, whether wild flowers or popular garden flowers, and soon garden areas were being set aside for flowers and foliage to be used in arrangements.

Perhaps the most noticeable impact on the garden was the inclusion of plants for foliage, whether architectural or in tones of greys and yellows. "Everlasting" flowers or flowers that could be easily dried also gained a new popularity, often undeserved by any actual contribution to an attractive flower border. For more exotic decorations, teasels, dried alliums and acanthus made surprise appearances, and whole borders were taken over by the often thuggish thalictrum and gypsophila, which, despite their delicate appearance, can spread alarmingly. Although perhaps the most popular, Constance Spry's were not the only books for the gardening flower arranger. In 1960, Violet Stevenson published *The Flower Arranger's Garden*, followed only seven years later by Jane Derbyshire's *The Flower Arranger and Her Garden*, both instructing how to bring the outdoors indoors, at a time when most people were determinedly taking the indoors outdoors.

ABOVE: Posing in the front garden of a 1930s semi, this woman seems to have more than flower arranging on her mind. .

LEFT: Coronation year inspired a new wave of bedding arrangement in public parks and even private front gardens, with bedding picked out in red, white and blue. Seen here at The Woods show garden, Chelsea Flower Show, 1953.

11

Going Wild with Decking

PREVIOUS PAGE: A popular wild-flower garden at Chelsea Flower Show in 1990. Gardens increasingly use wild flowers to add variety and interest as well as biodiversity.

RIGHT: John Chambers sells specific mixes of wild-flower seed as well as individual varieties. Miriam Rothschild was one of the founders of the wild-flower garden movement. Her mix for encouraging butterflies was originally grown on the tennis courts of her family home.

BELOW: Whether a result of the varroa mite, colony collapse, the absence of wild flowers or a combination of all three, bees are under threat and with them our gardens and our food source. Planting bee-friendly flowers and even wild flowers in the garden may help reverse this trend.

"Growing your own'" received a boost in the 1970s in the rather unexpected guise of a television soap opera. *The Good Life* followed the fortunes – or rather the lack of fortune – of a suburban couple who left the rat race to become self-sufficient. The tellingly named Tom and Barbara Good (played by Richard Briers and Felicity Kendal) transform their Surbiton, Surrey home and garden into a muddy and rather chaotic smallholding, growing all their own food and keeping hens and pigs. Their respectable neighbours, Jerry and Margot Leadbetter (played by Paul Eddington and Penelope Keith), are aghast both at the scene over their garden fence and at the seeming insanity of their neighbours. The programme ran for three years, 1975–78, and was phenomenally successful, with repeats still shown over 30 years later. In the USA, the series was transmitted as *Good Neighbors* which, unless chosen for its ironic twist, rather missed the point. In 2010 the Garden Museum mounted an exhibition entitled "The Good Life: 100 Years of Growing Your Own", taking the soap opera as inspiration for its title.

The early 1970s also saw the rather delayed coming of age of the Henry Doubleday Reseach Association (HDRA), now known by the rather more informal title "Garden Organic". The HDRA was founded in 1954 by

GOING WILD WITH DECKING

Lawrence Hills, an Essex horticulturalist and writer with a keen interest in the then fledgling organic movement. Named after a little-known Quaker smallholder called Henry Doubleday who had imported the extraordinarily heavy-cropping Russian comfrey (*Symphytum x uplandicum*), the HDRA went on to experiment with methods of composting and plant nutrition, including using comfrey as an organic compost and liquid feed. By 1973 the association's membership and experimental trials had expanded to such an extent that it needed full-time staff, and Alan and Jackie Gear (both scientists) were recruited. Eventually moving to Ryton-on-Dunsmore (Coventry) in 1986, the HDRA purchased nine hectares (22 acres) of land, where it still has its organic show gardens and demonstration plots. By 2010 the association had come from being regarded as an umbrella for gardening cranks and Luddites to being a highly regarded international research and development centre for the organic movement. With over 10 per cent of schools in the United Kingdom signing up to the renamed Garden Organic's free educational programme, the message that organic is good for future generations, and good for the Earth, is gaining adherents by the day.

As well as organic gardening, designers and gardeners began to pay more attention to the issue of climate change, and to plant with drought and extreme climate in mind. Beth Chatto became famous for her planting designs for dry gardens. Gardening in the arid zone of Essex, she created a garden which did not require any watering, even in the driest of summers. Further planting for different areas within her garden were created for woodland shade and water. Chatto's commitment to horticulture and "the right plant in the right place" has earned her gold medals at the Chelsea Flower Show, as well as an Honorary Doctorate of Science from Anglia Ruskin University. The overlap between gardening and science has become ever more important as gardeners grapple with the effects of climate change, and with possibly associated problems such as the dramatic decline in bees and some bird species. Gardening programmes and magazines now regularly feature tips for making gardens wildlife-friendly, and even recommend the sowing of wild flowers – known for centuries by the term "weeds"!

The Good Life was not a gardening programme as such, but by the 1980s and into the 1990s, media gardening, and media gardeners, abounded. *Gardeners' World*, a BBC production, filmed its first episode in 1968. It was originally presented by Percy Thrower and often featured his own garden at The Magnolias in Shrewsbury (Shropshire). Percy Thrower was followed by the less well-known Arthur Billet, who gave way to Geoff Hamilton, who was to be the face of 1980s gardening. For almost a decade, *Gardeners' World* became synonymous with Hamilton's garden at Barnsdale (Rutland), which eventually expanded to eight acres (3.25 hectares) of 38 themed gardens. Hamilton was an early advocate of organic gardening and, although *Gardeners' World* continued to feature advice which included chemical control of pests and insects, he helped to make the organic garden more mainstream.

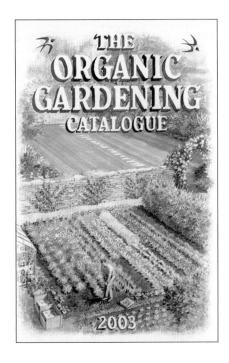

BELOW: Organic gardening has gained ground rapidly in response to concerns over genetic modification, chemical pollutants, decline in the bee population and climate change.

BOTTOM: Gardening for wildlife would have horrified gardeners of the wartime generation, who were determined to keep anything that moved out of the vegetable plot.

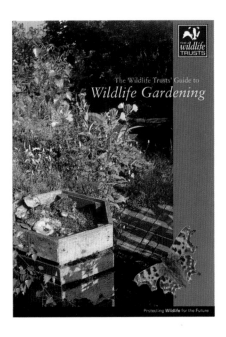

ABOVE: Percy Thrower was the first presenter of *Gardeners' World* and originator of the concept of the media gardener.

RIGHT: *Gardeners' World* spin-offs included one-off special programmes, magazines, websites, blogs, books, calendars and gardening wall planners.

BELOW: Sex raised its head in the garden with the advent of presenters such as Alan Titchmarsh, Monty Don and Charlie Dimmock, who attracted audiences that tuned in for the presenters as much as the plants!

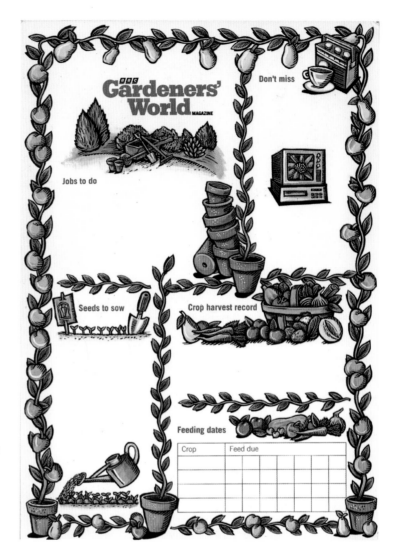

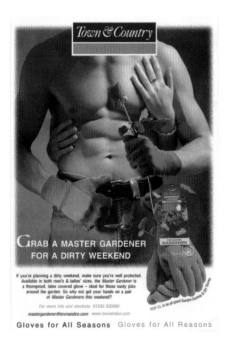

For many, however, it was the gentle Yorkshire dialect and broad smile of Alan Titchmarsh that sealed the place of the programme in the nation's hearts. First brought on to BBC to present a programme from the Chelsea Flower Show in 1983, Titchmarsh was a frequent but irregular presenter and guest on garden and chat shows until Geoff Hamilton's death in 1996, when he was brought in to present *Gardeners' World*. As media styles changed, a range of supporting presenters and guests were introduced to keep the programme "moving along" with frequent changes of scene and topic. Gay Search, who appeared alongside Geoff Hamilton from 1988, was the first female presenter, and her success cleared the way for Pippa Greenwood, Anne Swithinbank, Carol Klein and Rachel de Thame. A *Gardeners' World* magazine to accompany the programme was launched in 1991, and followers can now keep up to date via a website and presenters' blogs. As Alan Titchmarsh expanded beyond horticulture to become a heart-throb for many horticulturally minded women, gardening as a whole (or at least media gardening) benefited from his presence, and his "retirement" to take up novel writing and other media work in 2002

GOING WILD WITH DECKING

welcome to the world of
solardome ®

LEFT: A small-scale Eden! The first solardome glasshouse became available in 1969, and the company recently celebrated its fortieth anniversary.

BELOW: Better known for his vacuum cleaners and hand dryers, James Dyson patented the ballbarrow in 1974. Although manoeuvrable and colourful, it never caught on, but the occasional example may still be spotted lurking in a garden shed!

presented a problem, until the BBC lighted upon Monty Don. A professional broadcaster and journalist, already on a second career, Don's passion for gardening, and in particular organic and productive gardening, made him an ideal replacement. As the first presenter who had had no actual professional gardening training, he captured the spirit of the new century as the baby-boomer generation took to the plot.

Programmes such as *Gardeners' World*, and its radio counterpart *Gardeners' Question Time* (originating from a wartime broadcast, *How Does Your Garden Grow?*), approached gardening from a relatively traditionalist perspective, although organic gardening principals, recycling of materials and biological control of pests are increasingly highlighted, thanks to presenters such as the aptly named Bob Flowerdew. The 1990s saw a rush of "quick fix" and makeover gardening programmes that took their inspiration both from the prevailing mood of the country and the fashion for decking, hard landscaping and other instant features. Often presented within a largely artificial time limit, there was a race against time for presenters and helpers to excavate water features, investigate historic gardens, plant fully grown trees, lay paving and install summerhouses – all to the delight (or occasional dismay) of owners. Foremost amongst these programmes was *Ground Force*, with its winning combination of Alan Titchmarsh, Charlie Dimmock and the builder Tommy Walsh. Dimmock was almost equally popular with gardeners and non-gardeners, with an enticing combination of skill with water features and lack of bra. Other

BELOW: Like many traditional gardening tools, long-handled fruit pickers, designed to harvest apples and pears and then catch them in the bag, were given a modern twist in the twentieth century.

ABOVE: The Lost Gardens at Heligan awakened the public's interest in historic gardens, uniting a sense of mystery and discovery.

BELOW: The National Gardens Scheme, with its distinctive Yellow Book, has gone from strength to strength and now encompasses some 3,700 gardens.

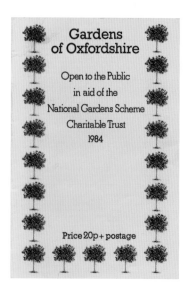

garden makeover programmes struggled against the overwhelming popularity of *Ground Force*, but variations on the theme created *Lost Gardens* (Channel 4, 1999–2001) and *Hidden Gardens* (BBC), in which historic gardens were researched and restored. More recently, *Garden Invaders* combined a horticultural quiz show and makeover, fronted by the 1980s pop star Kim Wilde and all filmed against the clock – perhaps the ultimate in combining television formats!

The television series *Lost Gardens* and *Hidden Gardens* were both responding to the public's increasing fascination with heritage gardens, and most especially the thrill of discovery and restoration. In 1990 Tim Smit and John Willis literally led the way as they hacked and fought their route through the brambles and sycamores on the Tremayne family's Cornish estate of Heligan. Although one could hardly describe the gardens of Heligan as "sleeping" through the decades since their abandonment, as the weeds had been particularly active and fecund, the garden had certainly been "lost" and almost totally forgotten. When clearance commenced, led by Smit and John Nelson and helped by BTCV (formerly known as British Trust for Conservation) volunteers, areas of formal garden re-emerged into the light. The Italian Garden was the first to be restored (in 1991), although the glasshousing and buildings of the Melon Yard had been uncovered the year before. The Vegetable Garden, the Flower Garden, and the aptly named Jungle Garden followed, along with the Sundial Garden and finally the Lost Valley. From its earliest days the site had attracted media attention, and it was open to visitors almost before the first restorations. Soon coach parties flocked to the site to be part of its unfolding story.

GOING WILD WITH DECKING

As restoration of the original gardens neared completion, the opportunity arose for other aspects of gardening to become incorporated into the tale of the Lost Gardens of Heligan. Wildlife gardening, organic gardening and local community involvement all form part of the ongoing Heligan concept and overlap in many ways with Tim Smit's other groundbreaking undertaking – the Eden Project. Described at the outset as gardening on a world scale, the Eden Project's distinctive domes have become home to biomes from rainforest to desert. Reminiscent of Joseph Paxton taking a water lily leaf for his inspiration for the Chatsworth "Great Stove" glasshouse, Tim Smit and his team took inspiration from a washing-up bubble to design the domes that could settle on the uneven surface of the disused chalk quarry at Bodelva, near St Austell. The project houses the largest "conservatories" in the world, structures at the cutting edge of architecture, which were developed to hold some of the most endangered plants as well as some of the most common. The humid biome is 790 feet (240 metres) long, 360 feet (110 metres) wide and 165 feet (50 metres) high, and contains a staggering 1,000 plant species. Over 9.5 million people have visited the Eden Project since its official opening in 2000, and 250 school children visit every day, taking home with them an idea of the wealth of plants that share the planet rather than just our gardens.

Garden visiting, first formalized in the eighteenth century, has now become a national obsession. The raising of money for charity sees more gardens

ABOVE: The First International Garden Festival was held in Liverpool in 1984. Sixty gardens covered the 10,226,000-square-foot (950,000-square-metre) site.

BELOW: This potager, designed by Rosemary Verey for her own garden at Barnsley House, draws on historic inspiration from Villandry, France, as well as modern design.

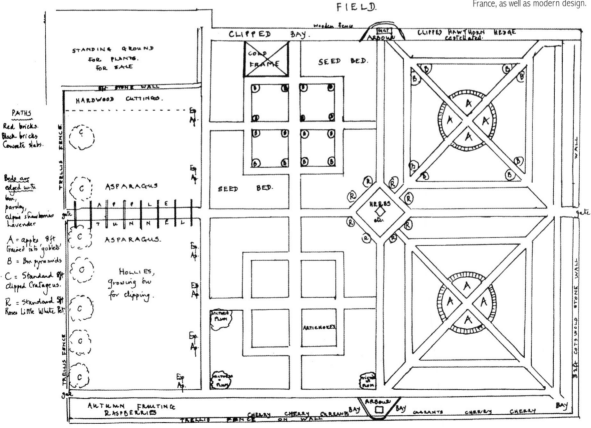

open each year, and there seems no limit to our passion for pottering in other people's borders. Over 3,700 gardens were listed as open in the National Gardens Scheme "Yellow Book" in 2010, with many more open as part of the British Red Cross Open Gardens. Numerous villages hold open gardens days, and other gardens open under individual initiatives for small or less well-known charities (my Cambridgeshire garden even opens in aid of the Rabbit Welfare Association!). In addition, the National Trust, now with more than 3.5 million members, maintains over 215 houses, many of them with historic gardens and parks. The Historic Houses Association (HHA), representing over 1,500 privately owned stately homes, castles and gardens (of which 300 are open to the public), runs a competition for a Garden of the Year, in association with Christies. Winners, decided by the HHA's 26,000 members, have included Kiftsgate Court (Gloucestershire), West Dean Gardens (Sussex), Hever Castle (Kent), Houghton Hall (Norfolk) and most recently Chenies Manor (Buckinghamshire), most of them combining historic gardens and structure with excellent modern design and planting. Alongside the rise of garden visiting, garden festivals and shows of all kinds have become increasingly popular. The most famous of them all, the RHS Chelsea Flower Show, now receives 160,000 visitors in its annual five days of opening.

Garden history has also come of age during the last 30 years, and 1977 saw the founding of the Museum of Garden History at Lambeth, housed in the redundant church of St Mary-at-Lambeth, adjacent to Lambeth Palace. The museum (later the Garden Museum) incorporated exhibitions, displays,

BELOW: The seventeenth-century-style garden at the Garden Museum, Lambeth houses the tombs of the John Tradescants and was designed by the Dowager Marchioness of Salisbury. John Tradescant the Elder worked at Hatfield, now the seat of the Salisburys, between 1610 and 1615.

OPPOSITE: Once the back garden was decked, the front garden was often paved to allow car parking. By 2010 this was being discouraged as it was thought to exacerbate problems with water run-off during rain storms and flash floods.

events and also a small garden in seventeenth-century style, incorporating the tomb of the John Tradescants (Elder and Younger), gardeners and plant collectors. In 1983 English Heritage produced the first Register of Parks and Gardens of Special Historic Interest, alerting planners and owners to the most important components of historic designed landscapes in their care. Since then, the list of registered sites has expanded to 1,600 and information is continually updated. The Garden History Society, founded in 1966, has also blossomed and now boasts over 1,500 members with an active role in research and conservation. County-based garden history trusts also exist for almost every county in England, whose members spend their weekends visiting, recording and enjoying historic gardens. As well as looking back to the designers and plant collectors of the past, these often vibrant societies work with schools to encourage "growing clubs" and reinstating school gardens where a future generation can explore the link between plot and plate.

As the twenty-first century dawned, decking was dividing the nation, embraced by some as the ultimate in instant, low-maintenance garden design, loathed by others as tantamount to concreting over the garden. The only profession united in its praise was private pest controllers – as the warm, dry space between boards and earth created a boom in the rat population. *Ground Force* was credited with helping to increase decking sales through its frequent use in featured gardens; sales of decking at the garden-hardware retailer B&Q rose from £5,000 in 1997 to £16 million in 2001. In an interview in the *Daily Mail*, Alan Titchmarsh was quoted as saying: "I am partly to blame for the decking boom, and I am sorry, I know it's everywhere these days."

Following on the heels of decking, or often placed on top of it, were a myriad of outdoor garden rooms, studios, summerhouses, garden offices and glorified sheds. In a variety of styles from log cabin to beach hut, Sussex shepherd shelter to New England settler, outdoor rooms became an essential as house prices rocketed and people extended their living area out, rather than move on. Making space for a real garden room often turned attention to garden design generally, and more specifically routes between house and garden room, rather perversely resulting in an expansion of vistas and routes, as well as a reduction in the traditional design of segmented areas traditionally known as garden rooms!

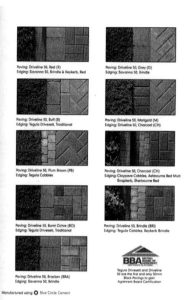

BELOW: In extreme cases entire gardens were decked over, with only pot plants left!

Perhaps related to the increase in paving and decking, sales of vegetable and flower seeds dipped during the 1980s and '90s, and by the time of the resurgence in the 2000s, some companies had found it hard going. Easily available pot-rooted plants appealed to a generation used to instant gratification, and even Woolworth, traditional sellers of cheap-and-cheerful seed packets from their Cuthbert's range, started to move into plug plants. Interviewed in 1997, Phil Kabane, the then gardening buyer for Woolworth, pointed out: "Many people who buy seeds, as opposed to plants, tend to be older, and they don't always have access to a car, so they still come to the high street for their shopping." With an unfortunate lack of foresight, he went on to say, "I don't foresee a time yet when we won't be carrying seeds in Woolworth's." In 2008 the chain went into administration and all 800 British shops were closed; the days of the technicolour stand of seed packets, full of promise and delight in the summer months, were no more.

The road was just as rocky for the seed companies. By the time Woolworth collapsed in 2008/9, Cuthbert's had already taken over both Dobie Mail Order Seeds and the famous Carters' Tested Seeds, and had in turn been acquired by a Swedish firm, eventually settling with Vilmorin, a giant French horticultural group. Seed Production, based in Torquay (Devon), was shared with Sutton's Seeds in 1997, although the historic Cuthbert's Seeds sold in Woolworth were by then actually marketed under licence rather than actually produced by Cuthbert's. It was a sad ending for so many of our historic seed merchants and companies, whose history can be traced back centuries.

As the credit crunch hit in 2009, gardeners responded by an increased emphasis on Grow Your Own, with many muttering about a return to Dig for Victory! Vegetable seeds once again outsold flower seeds, and allotments gained waiting lists unheard-of since the 1940s. Down on the allotment much has changed since its original heyday 70 years ago. In 1942 the government was proud to announce that out of more than a million allotments, 10,000 were held by women. In 2006 the number had increased to 59,000 plots out of 330,000 – almost a quarter. On some sites women now outnumber men, and more and more families can be seen enjoying a bit of productive family time. Concerns over genetic modification of foodstuffs, and the environmental consequences of food air-miles, have given renewed impetus to the fashion for the "good life" that started over 30 years ago. For those who cannot grow their own, "food boxes" can be delivered full of fresh produce grown in market gardens or local community gardens, whilst an increasing number of towns and cities have farmers' and smallholders' markets, encouraging small-scale business and direct sales, keeping food fresh and more hands on the land. They may not be gardens but every green space counts on this crowded island.

Not only vegetables responded to the credit crunch and banking collapses. Designers such as Tim Stuart Smith predicted a return to more formal and simplified garden design with high-maintenance herbaceous planting slimmed down and replaced by an emphasis on clean green and white lines; box hedging,

ABOVE: Many school gardens have been concreted over in response to the need for car parking and to concerns over health and safety for children engaged in gardening.

BELOW: In 1979, the Victoria and Albert Museum exhibition "The Garden: A Celebration of A Thousand Years of British Gardening" sparked a revival of interest in historic gardens and design. The then director of the V&A was Roy Strong, later to become president of the Garden History Society.

still water and cool paving creating areas of serenity and calm amidst the chaos and stress of modern living. Makeover gardens were predicted to give way to gardens where things grow and mature, the chequebook garden replaced by the traditional seedbed and compost heap. In 2009, Stephen Crisp, head gardener at the US Embassy in London, claimed that he would henceforth be spending time dividing up perennials, growing from cuttings, starting small and waiting for plants to grow – economical outlooks not usually associated with America, the consummate consumer.

Predictions for a more thoughtfully thrifty Chelsea Flower Show were, however, confounded in 2010 by the appearance of the "bling" garden. Containing (at least briefly) diamonds worth over 20 million pounds, David Domoney's "Ace of Diamonds" garden was publicized as a feelgood garden for those who had ridden out the recession, sparkling with gems and packed with flowers such as *Hosta* "Diamond Tiara", *Narcissus* "Diamond Ring" and *Potentilla* "Gold Finger". Perhaps ironically, the Ace of Diamonds garden only attained a bronze medal, rather than a coveted gold, silver-gilt or even silver. At the opposite end of the financial world, "Places of Change", a garden created in partnership between the Homes and Communities Agency, Homeless Link and the Eden Project, was awarded a silver medal.

ABOVE: The Wish Tree, from the "Places of Change" garden at Chelsea 2010. People were asked to write wishes and messages to form part of the garden.

BELOW: The famous Tony Blair gnome, housed at the Garden Museum, Lambeth. Politics and gardening are increasingly linked as issues relating to climate change, planning and conservation impact on gardens.

As roses bloomed in the late spring of 2010, news of forthcoming changes in planning legislation heralded a clampdown on building on garden sites. Altering the planning status of gardens from "brownfield", where they sat alongside derelict factories and car parks, to "greenfield" will mean that our gardens are saved for the next generation – an essential legacy for the future of our nation of gardeners.

The Garden Museum

Call it luck; call it fate, or what you will, but the fact that the Church of St Mary-at-Lambeth still stands on the banks of the Thames and that it now houses the Garden Museum seems rather like poetic justice. Fated in the mid 1970s to be demolished and turned into a coach park, it was thanks to the detective work and the determination of Rosemary Nicholson and her husband, John, that the church was preserved. The couple had been looking for a tomb in its burial ground belonging to two of the nation's greatest gardeners and plantsmen, John Tradescant and his son, another John.

Standing next door to Lambeth Palace, the church had already been deconsecrated in the mid 1970s when Rosemary and John established the Tradescant Trust in 1977 and set about restoring the church to turn it into the Museum of Garden History. Supported by various garden lovers, such as the late Queen Elizabeth the Queen Mother, HRH The Prince of Wales, and the Dowager Marchioness of Salisbury, who is its President, the Museum has garnered a collection of rare and fascinating artefacts and ephemera – everything from a Tudor watering pot to saucy postcards with gardening themes and seed packets from the 1950s and 60s, not to mention the odd tin of weedkiller!

Like a good garden, however, the Museum has evolved. In 2007, a competition was held to find a new design for the interior of the church, one that could showcase exhibitions to the public, and also allow the Museum to flourish as an arena for gardeners to discuss and enjoy their horticultural enthusiasms. Thus, in November 2008, the Museum of Garden History was reborn as the Garden Museum, reopening after its refurbishment.

Hosting a variety of events from talks to plant fairs and more, the Museum still offers visitors a chance to view the quirky and charming objects that it has collected over the years and the opportunity to visit the tombs of the Tradescants, who as collectors themselves, may no doubt look down and smile at the fact that, while today's gadgets might save on labour, good gardens are born of a passion that all the Museum's visitors share.

For details about opening times and how to find the Garden Museum and café, please visit the Museum's website: www.gardenmuseum.org.uk

Bibliography

A Thing in Disguise; The Visionary Life of Joseph Paxton, Kate Colquhoun, Fourth Estate, 2003

Allotments, Twigs Way, Shire Publications, Oxford, 2008

Ancient Roman Gardens, Linda Farrar, Sutton Publishing, 2000

Beauties of a Cottage Garden, The, Gertrude Jekyll, Penguin, London, 2009

Children and Gardens, Gertrude Jekyll, Antique Collectors Club, 1982

Dig on for Victory: Mr Middleton's All-year-round Gardening Guide from 1945, C H Middleton, Aurum Press Ltd, London, 2009

Digging for Victory: Gardens and Gardening in Wartime Britain, Twigs Way, Sabrestorm Publishing, 2010

Edwardian Garden, The, David Ottewill, Yale University Press, London, 1989

English Garden, The, Ursula Buchan and Andrew Lawson, Frances Lincoln, London, 2006

Flora: An Illustrated History of the Garden Flower, Brent Elliott and Sir Simon Hornby, Scriptum-Cartago, 2002

Garden Triumphant: A Victorian Legacy, David Stuart, Viking, 1988

Gardening Women: Their Stories from 1600 to the Present Day, Catherine Horwood, Virago Press 2010

Gardens of Gertrude Jekyll, The, Richard Bisgrove, Frances Lincoln, London, 1992

Gardens of the National Trust, Stephen Lacey, National Trust, 2005

Head Gardeners, The, Toby Musgrave, Aurum Press 2007

In Your Garden, Vita Sackville-West, Frances Lincoln (re-issue), London, 2004

Little History of British Gardening, A, Jenny Uglow, Pimlico, London, 2005

Lost Gardens of Heligan, The, Tim Smit, Channel Four, London, 1998

Medieval Garden, The, Sylvia Landsberg, The British Museum, London, 1998

My Lifetime of Gardening, Percy Thrower, Littlehampton Books, 1977

New Shoots Old Tips, Caroline Holmes, Frances Lincoln, London, 2004

Origin of Plants, The: The People and Plants That Have Shaped Britain's Garden History Since the Year 1000, Maggie Campbell-Culver, Headline, London, 2001

Plant Hunters, The, Carolyn Fry, Andre Deutsch, London, 2009

Plants in Garden History, Penelope Hobhouse, Pavilion Books, London, 2004

Pursuit of Paradise, The: A social History of Gardens and Gardening, Jane Brown, HarperCollins, London, 2000

Regency Gardens, Mavis Batey, Shire Publications, Oxford, 1995

Royal Gardeners, Alan Titchmarsh, BBC Books, London, 2003

Royal Horticultural Society, The: a History, Brent Elliott, Phillimore & Co Ltd, 2004

Victorian Gardener, The : The Growth of Gardening and the Floral World, Anne Wilkinson, Sutton Publishing, 2006

WEBSITES

English Heritage: www.english-heritage.org.uk
Parks and Gardens UK: www.parksandgardens.ac.uk
The Garden History Society: www.gardenhistorysociety.org
The Garden Museum: www.gardenmuseum.org.uk
The National Gardens Scheme: www.ngs.org.uk
The National Trust: www.nationaltrust.org.uk

Index

Credits

PUBLISHERS' CREDITS

The publishers would like to thank Philip Norman at the Garden Museum for the inordinate amount of help he provided in finding material in the Museum's archives, his expert advice and for his support of the project. Thanks are also due to the Museum's Director, Christopher Woodward, and Mary Guyatt, the Curator, for their support and timely help.

PUBLISHING CREDITS

Editorial Manager: Vanessa Daubney
Additional editorial work: Philip Parker, Catherine Rubinstein and Gemma Maclagan
Art Director: Sooky Choi
Additional design work: Lucy Parissi; Katie Baxendale and Kate Painter
Picture Researcher: Jenny Meredith
Production Controller: Rachel Burgess